Once Upon a Wartime

Peter Layton Cottingham

Printed in Canada by
Leech Printing
Brandon, Manitoba, Canada

Designed by
Prairie Mountain Publishers Inc.
Brandon, Manitoba, Canada

Special thank you to Velma Clayton and David Cottingham for their editing assistance, and to my friend Herb Peppard, for his advice and support.

Cover photo taken at Grasse, France in August, 1944.

Canadian Cataloguing in Publication Data

Cottingham, Peter Layton, 1921-
    Once upon a wartime

Rev. ed.
ISBN 0-9680969-1-3

1. Cottingham, Peter Layton, 1921-
2. First Special Service Force — Biography.
3. World War, 1939-1945 — Personal narratives, Canadian. I. Title.

D811.C68 1996a   940.54'1271   C96-901012-5

Dedication

This collection of memories is dedicated with deepest love and affection to the memory of my dear wife, Muriel Margaret (Gill) Cottingham.

Without her gentle persuasion, and at times, misplaced faith in my ability as a writer of sorts, this book would not have been attempted.

Contents

Foreword

At the urging of my dear wife Muriel, I have been persuaded to catalogue, in some semblance of order, the highlights of the rather unusual three score and ten which have, so far, been my happy allotment. That has given me an excuse, if such were really needed, to submit to a primordial instinct to leave some record of a life which I would not have exchanged for any other. This is not to say, that given other circumstances, I may have lived my life differently. Had I done so, what I have to offer in this small volume may have been dull fare indeed. Perhaps the same forces move me to relate my tale here as those which persuaded the hunters and gatherers of earlier times to leave drawings of their exploits on the walls of their caves.

In the writing of these memoirs I have had to draw on memories, some of which are almost too painful to recall. Others, in varying degrees, have helped me to put my life into some kind of perspective which I find is a form of catharsis in the healing of my mind. Some war veterans express a reluctance to relate any of the details of the battles they may have been in. In some cases they use that as an excuse for not having been in any battles. That is understandable and forgivable and should not cause anyone to have a feeling of guilt or embarrassment.

A lot of brave men and women served in the Forces of our country. They didn't all manage to tangle at first hand with the enemy, but our victory could not have been achieved without their many vital contributions. In the main, I would suggest that many of the battle situations that a lot of veterans experienced were, in fact, far too painful to relive in the telling. I have personally witnessed the complete destruction of tanks, planes, landing craft and ships. During those traumatic times I was selfishly relieved that someone other than I was occupying them.

I must admit that in my case I was blessed (or cursed) with an ability to detach myself to some extent from the mayhem which went on around me. It may have been that which saved what mental stability I may have been able to exhibit from time to time. There had to be some form of selfish inborn ability to survive which carried me throughout the war. There were very few times when I considered myself in any way valorous. The only times I even came close were in moments of great stress when I must have done the right thing and cannot to this day imagine what propelled me. Most of the time, such as when we were undergoing an intense artillery barrage, I cringed in mortal terror hoping to be spared the fate of some of the men around me who were not so fortunate.

I believe that Winston Churchill, who had his own share of wars to live through, knew what he was talking about. He said that each man has his own store of courage and when that is used up he has no more to draw on. The Army had owned my body and soul for over five years when the atomic bombs were dropped on Japan in August of 1945. I hope the reader will forgive the euphoria that I experienced when I realised that I no longer had to look forward in dread to fighting in the jungles of Burma. My supply of whatever courage I had may possibly have run dry.

My experiences during the war exist in my memory as something that I could not possibly have missed. It was such an all encompassing event that to have been left out of it I would have considered myself forever deprived. I would always have been left to wonder, "Did I have what it takes to make a man part of the march of history?"

In retrospect, I would suggest that the war which was to make such an indelible imprint on my total being actually began in August of 1914. I am glad that I wasn't born until at least three years after the really tough part of it had been temporarily suspended on the 11th of November, 1918. At that time everyone was so war weary that it was hopefully described as "The War to End all Wars." It is my firm belief that it was just a truce to allow each side a breather in which to produce a new generation of "cannon fodder" and upgrade the weaponry. Unfortunately the country which did most of the upgrading was Germany in spite of the restrictions imposed on them by the Treaty of Versailles.

My father, an adventurous young Englishman, had been lured to the Swan River Valley in 1911. At that time it was considered to be in Northern Manitoba. Posters in British travel agencies portrayed Western Canada as the land of golden harvests and countless other attractions. There appeared to be endless opportunities for anyone with the courage and determination to escape from the smokestacks of industrial Britain. Thus it was that he began his life in Canada as a farm hand in the Valley. He worked on a beautiful farm which was bordered on the north by a winding and full flowing crystal clear stream known as the Swan River.

Homesteads were still available in the Valley and could be obtained for the great sum of ten dollars. A homestead consisted of one hundred and sixty acres of virgin territory, mostly bush. Father managed to purchase one with the proviso that he erect a dwelling on it within a certain period of time. In so doing he could be granted full title to the land. The Valley had been gaining a reputation for its fine farmland. Aside from the depth and richness of its soil it was difficult to find a stone on any of its acreage. The forest itself contained wealth in timber waiting for someone to make use of that resource as well.

In Father's spare time he managed to erect a basic three-roomed log house on his homestead and thereby qualify as a man of property. No sooner had he met that condition than he learned that his mother country, Britain, was at war with Germany. When Canada followed suit and declared war on the mutual enemy he couldn't resist the call to arms and volunteered his services as an infantry-man. After an obscenely short period of training in Canada he and his regiment were shipped overseas to become involved in the ter-rible slaughter of trench warfare in France.

In due course he was severely wounded. Mail directed to him was marked "Killed (in) Action." However, someone in battalion headquarters knew that he was still alive when he passed through the regiment's aid post. His mail was redirected to a hospital in England where it finally reached him. His dreams of golden har-vests were put on hold.

Following a long and painful convalescence Father met and married Anne Henrietta Macara Layton, the beautiᵢ daughter of a stern Methodist minister in Nova Scotia. During his recovery he had learned the trade of telegraphy and was hired by the Canadian National Railway as an operator. Employment on the railway, although it paid a living wage, was subject to insecurity as to loca-tion because of the system of seniority. Without the seniority to hold a steady job he was moved about for the first few years of their marriage. Thus it was that after several years experience in Nova Scotia an opening for an operator appeared at Swan River in Manitoba. Father could see his dream unfold as he would be able to earn a living with his newly acquired vocation and live on his own property at the same time. In true pioneer spirit he moved his wife and infant son, David, who was born in Halifax, out to his log cabin in the Swan River Valley.

It is difficult to imagine conditions more primitive than those under which my dear mother delivered me into this world. I was born in Father's log cabin in what was then a densely forested part of the Canadian wilderness. The nearest community of any account was a pioneer settlement, the town of Swan River, some five miles distant.

On the twenty-third of November in 1921 the Swan River Valley was well into a winter which was notable for the depth of its snow and the severity of its cold. The day my delivery was imminent my father set off on horseback through the deep snow in an attempt to find a doctor in the town. I was born during his absence. My mother had a neighbour woman who was supposedly there to assist in my birth. My mother claimed that the woman refused to touch me. The cabin also lacked the conveniences we now take for granted such as indoor plumbing, telephone, electricity and central heat. On the plus side no one had to pay for a doctor as none could be found on such short notice. Mother and I survived regardless. What a remarkable woman she was.

Some time after my first birthday Father was again moved by the railway. He was given a station back east in Nova Scotia. It was during that period that my younger brother, Rick, was born. Another Nova Scotian. When Rick was almost two we moved again to a very interesting place for me and my brothers, if not for my parents. That place was Superior Junction, in Northern Ontario. It was so named as it was the key spot on the C.N.R. main line where all the trains from the west which were bound for the inland ports of Port Arthur and Fort William, now known as Thunder Bay, had to branch off and head for the north shore of Lake Superior. My first memories are of life at Superior Junction.

The junction was the first station east of Sioux Lookout, Ontario. It was most vital to the Canadian transportation system at the time. There was no trans Canada highway nor was there any such thing as Trans Canada Airlines. It may be noted that in those days Sioux Lookout was the busiest hub of air transportation in North America. There were more landings and take-offs at Sioux Lookout than either New York or Chicago could boast. Its airport consisted of a large lake from which the many float planes in summer and ski-equipped planes in winter catered to the frenzied traffic of the greatest gold rush in Canadian history. The many mines in the Laurentian Shield of Northern Ontario were being developed. Many of them are still in full production.

When my father was posted to Superior Junction the living accommodations for his family were not yet available so the railway placed a "bunk car" on a side track about one hundred yards east of the station. There was usually a string of empty box cars on the same side track between the bunk car and the station. We were to live in that primitive environment until the former occupant of the station's living quarters vacated same. It was during that period that I had two very good chances to end my brief career.

On the first occasion I was left in the care of my father at his office in the station. He could not leave his desk as there was always train order traffic on the telegraph which had to be monitored and in many cases acted upon.

In spite of his instructions that I must under no circumstances wander away from his office, I managed to sneak down to the river bank behind the station. Water must have a compelling attraction for small boys, so many of them are led astray by its appeal.

I found a dock of sorts which jutted out into the river. I walked out on it to have a better look into the mysterious depths of the water which flowed clear and inviting. Perhaps I expected to see some fish. As I stood on one particular board it appeared to be nailed at only one end. The end I was standing on tipped forward dumping me into the water. I must have learned to swim in that brief dunking as I made it to the shore. An involuntary dog-paddle, no doubt.

As I squished my sodden way into my father's office I was certain that I was about to feel the full fury of his fatherly concern. He didn't let me down—just my pants. My father loved me and wanted me to survive. It dawned on me that he really did know best. That spanking did more for me than any tongue lashing could have possibly accomplished. They say, "Curiosity killed the cat." I have wondered many times since, "How many four-year-olds has it killed ?"

On another occasion I had been visiting my father in his office and was making my way innocently down the tracks on my way 'home." I sauntered along unconcerned when I heard a train starting up behind me. I guess that I had just assumed that it was on the branch line to my right, which for several hundred yards ran parallel to the tracks on which I was walking. It was a freight train and most of them took the branch line to the Lakehead. I had almost reached our family "bunk car" when a man jumped out from between a couple of box cars to my left yelling and waving for me to get off the track. I did so with a hasty sideways jump as the train ran past. I seem to recall that for several weeks after that I had nightmares of trains chasing me.

One other event which happened at the "Junction" is worthy of note. Early fall was known as the "grain rush" as most of the traffic was composed of freight trains loaded with grain and headed for the huge terminals at the Lakehead. Interspersed with all of the grain trains were the four transcontinental passenger trains. Two were westbound and two were eastbound. They all passed through Superior Junction without even slowing down unless they were ordered to stop for some emergency for which they would have been alerted long before reaching the Junction.

My father, obliging fellow that he was, had been conned by the crews of the grain trains into leaving his desk to close the switch after trains had gone through on their way to the ports. That would eliminate them having to stop the train for the tail end brakeman to get off and close the switch. On the night in question my father had been on duty at his desk for over forty-eight hours without any sleep. He had wired the dispatcher in Winnipeg several times to alert him to the danger to the system if he happened to doze off. His pleas for a relief operator were unanswered for some reason and he was having a hard time staying awake.

He finally dozed off. He was rudely awakened by the shrill and urgent sound of a train whistle. He looked up in horror as he saw a row of lights coming around the curve about a half-mile to his west. They were the well-lit windows of a passenger train, probably doing over sixty miles per hour. The light on the switch at the end of the station platform was glowing an ominous red, signifying an open switch. He realised in a flash that while he was sleeping a freight train had passed through on its way to the ports. The train crew which had opened the switch expected him to close it the same as he usually did.

He sprinted from his office running as hard as he could to the switch at the end of the platform. The entire lower parts of the train were by that time illuminated by the sparks from the brakes at every wheel as the engine crew had activated the air brakes on every coach.

He swung the lever on the switch a second before the train rushed past with the fireman shaking his fist out the window of the cab. He had just managed to avert a terrible wreck. The crew may not have realised that a very brave man saved them all from a horrible death. One second later and the train could have wiped out my father, the station and everyone in it, and almost certainly would have resulted in fatalities to some of the crew and passengers. Father's act of heroism, although it became legendary among the train crews, could not receive any recognition from the railway as the ultimate responsibility for closing the switch rested with the crew of the freight train. For that reason it was never officially dealt with.

Our next move was to the most idyllic place which I can remember. I cannot recall anywhere in my many travels which more closely resembled my idea of heaven than Allenwater, a station about seventy-five miles east of the Junction. The country around Allenwater very much resembled that portrayed by many of the paintings of the Canadian artists known as the Group of Seven—the evergreen forests, the gin-clear lakes, the moss-covered rocks of the Laurentian Shield, and yes, the unspoiled Native population. They all lent a never-never-land aura to my recollections of that beautiful spot. I learned to fish and hunt and trap the odd rabbit from one of my Indian chums who lived on the west shore of our lake.

He often walked the mile down the tracks to the village school-house with me and my brothers. His family and others in the area were so kindly, and industrious in their own way at living off that beautiful land. They required no government handouts and seemed to be the most happy people I have ever encountered. Father bought snowshoes and moccasins for us which they skillfully fashioned. To this day I love the smell of a deerskin moccasin.

During the few years we spent in Allenwater we got to know many of the bush pilots who were flying from our lake into the gold mining country to the north. During the summers there were also a fair number of American sportsmen who flew in to enjoy the pristine lakes and the fabulous fishing in the area. One of our friends had a fly-in camp on a star-shaped island about three or four miles south of us. It was a five-sided island with every side a beautifully curved white sand beach. The island was wooded with spruce, birch and cedar trees and the lack of underbrush made it resemble the park on an English estate. It was a natural paradise if ever I saw one. Canoeing in the waters surrounding it we could see large fish swimming twenty and thirty feet below us. The water was that clear.

One day in particular sticks in my memory. It was like a scene from Dante's Inferno. There was a large forest fire burning about thirty miles west of us and the sky was so dark with smoke that in the few glimpses we had of the sun it was a dark red. The wind was more than gale force and the teacher let us out of school early because there was a danger of the fire reaching our homes if the wind stayed in the west as strong as it was. There was a great sense of foreboding.

As we made our way home from school along the track we had to traverse a land fill which was constructed across a narrow part of our lake. In crossing the narrows we were shocked to see one of the planes which normally flew a few times a week up to the mines. It was upside down and floating on its wings with the tail and pontoons up in the air at an angle. The wind had driven it into a cove near a beach on the east side of the lake. The waves were higher than we had ever seen them. The whole scene filled us with dread as we were concerned with the pilot's safety. We didn't actually know him but we knew his small son who attended school with us.

On reaching our home in the Allenwater station Mother was quite upset and told us that the Indians had been watching the plane land through their binoculars and had seen the wind blow it over and was forcing it across the lake. They came over to see if my father could be of help in trying to rescue the pilot. My older brother, David, wasn't feeling well that morning so stayed home from school. Father enlisted his help in going for his boat which was tied up in the shelter of a river mouth at the edge of the lake. He wanted David to accompany him because he was having trouble with the water pump which helped to cool its inboard motor. He had David pour cold water on the motor from time to time to keep it from overheating.

We all waited expectantly for Father's and David's safe return as we knew what the waves looked like that terrible afternoon. They made it across the lake and by the time they reached the plane it was near the far shore with the engine nose down in the sand in about five feet of water. Father dived in and determined that there was no one in the cockpit. He and David beached the boat with some difficulty in the high surf. They opted to walk home by way of the land fill and the railway track. The boat could wait for a calmer day.

The pilot's body was found after three days of dragging grappling hooks across the lake bottom near the area where the Indians had seen the plane capsize. Our small community was shaken by the loss of that man. Strangely, our beautiful lake didn't hold the same appeal in my young mind and for quite some time float planes had a different niche in my mental catalogue of interesting objects. It was my first encounter with a tragic death.

During our years in Northern Ontario our family grew by three more members. My brothers, Francis, Duncan and Paul were born. We had all looked forward to having at least one sister, but such was not to be. In the event of Paul's birth in Winnipeg, some operator who knew of my father's five sons, was to notify my father of the new arrival by wire. The clown took it upon himself to substitute the word daughter for son in announcing the birth. It took us all quite some time to forgive poor Paul for not being the girl we had all looked forward to meeting. We did, however, have the makings of a hockey team.

Toward the end of the "Roaring Twenties" as that decade was known, my father received an interesting proposition from an old prospector who was well known to him. He explained that he knew where there was a very strong outcropping of chromium ore. He had many samples to prove it. His deal was that Father would give him enough money to buy the supplies he needed for a couple of months in the bush. He would take his dog team back to the site and stake their claim to the ore rich property. Father's putting up the money for the venture was known as "grubstaking."

Father was to become his partner in any sale they would be able to make to a mining company. It was a risky business but the rewards were great if they should happen to strike it right. After a couple of months in the bush, staking and mapping, the prospector came out with plenty of evidence of a substantial claim. He and my father went off to Toronto to meet with the mining men and their geologist advisors. They were able to sell the property to the Chromium Mining and Smelting Corporation of Sault Ste. Marie, Michigan. The price they received in shares and cash was such as to enable Father to have a new home built on his homestead in Manitoba.

Our family moved to the Swan River Valley and began our lives as Manitobans. Father stayed in the employ of the railway for several years using the homestead as his base of operations and only accepting part-time work as a relief operator in the west. The money and shares he received from the chromium venture did much to enhance our family's lifestyle during the lean years of the thirties.

The few years we spent on the farm are not recalled with much joy. We missed the beautiful lake country of Northern Ontario. Our school was five miles distant in the town of Swan River and there were no such things as school busses in those days. I learned to hate the darkness of early morning preparations for the drive to school in the winters. The horse had to be led from the barn to the water trough after the ice was chopped away so he could get at the water. We harnessed him by lantern light and stuck a large sheaf of oats into the rack on the back of our cutter for his midday meal.

The five miles to school were often made longer by the huge snow drifts that we had to plow through at times. There was no such thing as insulated winter wear for children. I recall the many times when our hands were so cold that we could hardly manage to unhitch the horse and put him into the school stable. Another factor we had to live with was the reluctance of the school board to be concerned with the stable. They had no one detailed to clean out the barn and by the time school was out at four o'clock the manure behind the horses was frozen solid. By spring the horses were almost standing on their heads. I'm sure they were glad to welcome the spring thaws, as were we.

Life became a little better when we moved into town after about five years on the farm. Father had been appointed postmaster for the town and districts. Our house was just across the street from the school. We didn't usually leave for school until the bell rang. Quite a change from the five miles we had driven winter and summer.

The school in Swan River was a large brick building of three floors. The lowest floor, in a fairly dark basement, contained grades one, two and three. Imagine sending your children to school in something slightly better than a dungeon. The kids had to work their way up as they graduated to the higher grades. There was no electricity in the school although the town boasted a diesel plant which supplied power to the homes, businesses and the hospital. There was also no infrastructure for water and sewer. Indoor plumbing was only available to anyone lucky or wealthy enough to have a good well and a lot on the river bank. That was why one of the swimming holes was referred to as "sewer beach.'

In the late thirties I was sent to a boarding school in Winnipeg. It was St. John's College School at the corner of Church Avenue and Main Street in the north end. It was run on the same system as the "public" schools in England. They had strict dress and deportment codes which were religiously enforced. The school was an institution of the Anglican Church. There was chapel in the morning and evening and a compulsory study period prior to breakfast and another following the evening meal. They stressed physical fitness and the sports of hockey, football, tennis and some (optional) fencing. We also had a cadet corps in which we were taught World War I drill by a retired sergeant major.

While I was at St. John's, war clouds were forming over Europe. One of our school masters was very much up on current affairs. He predicted that Adolph Hitler, the Nazi chancellor of Germany, would drag us all into a horrible war. I was later to marvel at his foresight.

— Peter Layton Cottingham

CHAPTER 1

Once Upon a Wartime

Worm War I, also known as the Great War, had only ended a mere three years and twelve days before I was born. The Armistice, which was signed by the countries involved in World War I, had apparently given both sides a "breather" in order to regroup and rearm to continue the battle with new men and new weapons. It took them a mere twenty -two years to do just that. In 1939, Germany, then led by Adolph Hitler, was far better prepared to resume fighting than were any of the others.

They had literally thumbed their noses at the terms of the Treaty of Versailles and dared the Allies to interfere as they feverishly and openly rearmed. In so doing they developed a most imposing array of Twentieth Century armaments which included the largest air force in the world. The National Socialists, better known as Nazis, were planning great things for the Germany which was so badly beaten in World War I.

In September of 1939 Hitler ordered his huge, well trained and superbly equipped army and air force, to attack his neighbour to the East, Poland. His highly mechanized panzer divisions and swarms of dive bombers soon had most of Poland completely under German control. The ruthless rape and pillage of that country was a sickening prelude of things to come.

In the fall of 1939 many young Canadians were giving much thought to enlisting in one of the three services. We had a choice of the Army, the Royal Canadian Air Force or the Navy. I and several of my friends heard that there was an Air Force recruiting depot in Regina which was open for business. I managed to persuade my father to lend us his car for a trip to Regina in spite of the fact that he had put it away for the winter and had cancelled his insurance. Our trip to Regina ended in a minor disaster as we were unable to join the Air Force at that particular time.

On our way home I was driving too fast on a gravel road and had a blow-out in the right front tire. We were fortunate to survive with only minor injuries as even the best of cars were too hard to control when a front tire blew. I was unable to keep the car on the road and narrowly missed a hydro pole. The car scraped all of the rocks away from the base of the pole, badly damaging the right front fender and undercarriage. Father was the biggest loser in all of that. It cost him an "arm and a leg" to have the car repaired.

In the spring of 1940 Hitler and his minions turned their greedy eyes westward and with the same ruthless tactics began to overrun Holland, Belgium and France. And as a prelude to invading Britain their bombers were laying waste large sections of cities in the British Isles, London taking the worst of it. By June of 1940 things were looking very grim for chances of stopping the German onslaught. Very few men of military age were not moved to try to do something to stop what appeared to be the end of civilized life for the Western World as we knew it.

On a Saturday evening in early June my friends and I met at the stockyards just south of the railway station in our home town, Swan River, Manitoba. Our plan was to board one of the stock cars which were loading cattle for their trip to the abattoirs of Winnipeg. Money for tickets was almost non-existent in those days as we were just at the end of what was known as the Great Depression. Hence "riding the rods" (stealing a ride on a freight train) was a popular mode of travel for many of my generation at the time.

After dark we boarded the train by climbing through an opening at the end of the car as the side door through which the cattle were loaded was closed and sealed. The inside of a stock car contained feed racks on both sides which were above the heads of the cattle and had wide enough bars which held the hay.

The cattle were able to pull hay out through the bars. That presumably kept them from losing too much weight on their way to slaughter. The hay also made a rough bed for those of us who chose that type of transportation. Being young and in the company of good friends made the whole eighteen-hour trip to Winnipeg just another adventure some of us could laugh about in years to come.

We managed to extricate ourselves from our "side door Pullman" as the train slowed for entry into the city yards. In catching a transit bus for downtown the occupants of same appeared to notice our barn-like odour. We were treated to some very strange looks.

The next day I made my way to the R.C.A.F. recruiting office with a highly supportive reference letter extolling my mathematical qualifications. It was signed by my high school teacher and good friend, Ned French. He was sure that they could use someone of my potential.

It was the first of many occasions that fate intervened for good or ill. I was told that the Air Force, as much as they admired my qualifications, would have to do without my services for at least two whole weeks. They had all the bodies they could handle at the time. As mentioned, money was a problem in those days and I couldn't see my way clear to affording even the most basic food and housing for that length of time in the city of Winnipeg. In retrospect, had I managed to join the Air Force, the odds were that by mid 1942 or earlier I would most certainly have been resting quietly at the bottom of the English Channel, or in some well cared for site in Holland. It was not to be.

On exiting the front doors of the RCAF recruiting office I bumped into some of my Swan River friends who had recently joined the Princess Patricia's Canadian Light Infantry. They began to extoll the virtues of their regiment, telling me it was one of

Canada's finest fighting units with a great record of accomplishments in World War 1.

My father before me had been an infantryman in that war and hadn't fared very well to put it mildly. He received a wound so severe that his mail was returned to his battalion headquarters by his trench mates who swore that he was carried out dead. I have an envelope which was addressed to him in France by a woman in Swan River. It was marked "Killed in Action." The letter subsequently followed him to a military hospital in England where his recovery was long and extremely painful. He suffered from that wound for the rest of his life and died at the age of sixty-nine.

My friends persuaded me to come out to Fort Osborne Barracks and look the situation over. I have no knowledge of any bounty being offered for recruiting unsuspecting bodies into the infantry but there certainly should have been. In any event I was welcomed with open arms by the head honcho in the recruiting office who happened to be a Lieut. Colonel. His demeanor was quick to change after he had my name on the dotted line. I was tempted then to tell him that I had lied about my age and that he didn't really own me body and soul, as he then proceeded to indicate in a much less friendly manner.

Having had a "stretch" in the prison-like environment of St. John's College School in North Winnipeg during my high school years I was fairly well prepared for the restrictive measures which the army was about to inflict upon me. I had even had the basic army drill as a member of the St. John's Cadet Corps. Because of that I didn't find the regimentation too hard to take. Little did I suspect at the time that the army would indeed own me for the next five and a half years.

CHAPTER 2

The Transformation

The Rites of Passage in the metamorphic transition of an eighteen-year-old boy from a civilian into a trained soldier are indeed an exercise in enlightenment. It soon became painfully clear to me that I had signed away all of my rights as an individual with the exception of the right, presumably, to die for my country.

Under the guidance of an obnoxious NCO I was paraded over to a medical examination room. A team of doctors, in the uniforms of officers, were working on an assembly line of naked yokels such as myself. I was soon relieved of my civilian finery, and joined the line-up of inductees. It appeared that each of the examining staff had his own specialty depending on which part of the human body or mind was his particular study. I am sure that one of the doctors looked into my right ear with a light and, failing to see the room on the other side of my head, considered me to be of sound mind. Various other indignities too personal to mention were also performed on my person as I passed through the remaining stages of the line.

It may be of interest to note that one particular doctor asked me who had given me an appendectomy scar. I told him that a Doctor Stirling had operated on me in the Misericordia Hospital in Winnipeg when I was seven years old. He seemed almost friendly after that and revealed that he was Doctor Stirling. He had really saved my life as I had taken seriously ill with an inflamed appendix while living over three hundred miles from Winnipeg. Father was able to stop one of the transcontinental trains in the middle of the night which deposited my mother and me in Winnipeg in the morning.

The medical staff seemed to be satisfied with my mind and body as I was handed over to the obnoxious NCO and wheeled over to the Quartermaster Stores. I subsequently joined another long line of bodies waiting to be outfitted in the "King's Burlap" as the uniforms were referred to. I found out what the term "hair shirt" really meant. I also quickly learned that an army boot was about four times as heavy as the oxfords I had been wearing on my tender feet.

Along the line I was also issued with a gas mask (respirator), a steel helmet, circa 1914, a haversack with shoulder straps and a back pack about three times as big as the haversack. To further encumber me in my travels I was issued a water bottle, possibly pre-dating the "Charge of The Light Brigade." Some more webbing included items such as gaiters, belt, and two ammo pouches big enough to hold several Bren gun magazines in each. To top it all off I was handed two weapons which, when properly joined, became a .303 Lee Enfield rifle and bayonet. The latter may have seen service in the Boer War circa 1900. I recall being appalled at the thought of ever having to use a bayonet.

Socks, underwear, wedge cap, first aid package, razor and tooth brush almost completed my kit. For identification we were all issued a P.P.C.L.I. brass badge, red and white shoulder flashes with the same, sometimes obscenely translated, initials. I was later to be issued a rubber ground sheet which occasionally did duty as a poncho in the rain as well as something to sleep on during manoeuvres. Much later, I think it may have been during my time in Britain I was issued a gas cape. It was to be worn rolled up on top of our haversacks as part of proper battle dress equipment. I learned to hate the extra weight of something I would be reluctant to use even in the unlikely event of any gas attack.

Basic training at Fort Osborne consisted of much drill on the parade square. I was to learn that the P.P.C.L.I., as the Princess Pats were known, were peacetime permanent force army. Not to be confused with the militia who were known as Saturday Night Soldiers. As such they were meaner and leaner about military discipline and had a very high standard of expectations when it came to deportment, dress and drill.

I recall that it was the only outfit (out of the four that I would experience) in which a lousy corporal had enough power to administer the penalty of "Pack Drill" for a minor misdemeanor such as telling him to drop dead. They really meant business. I couldn't believe the army would create corporals out of some of the low lifes whose only claim to fame was their ability to polish apples and kiss butt. I had the nerve to suggest to one of our corporals that his mother was unlikely married to his father. As a result I found myself in full marching order, complete with steel helmet, full pack, gas mask, ammo pouches and rifle lined up in a squad of similar screw-ups after the evening meal.

After marching back and forth for a couple of hours at the slope arms on a drill square made of crushed cinders my right hand was so swollen that I couldn't make a fist. If that was pack drill I would try to avoid it from then on. I was soon to learn that the word "deportment" as practised by our instructors only referred to conduct in the confines of military jurisdiction. What a bunch of "alley cats" they were in their off-duty hours.

Besides a lot of drill we received intensive instruction in the use of weapons. I was impressed with the genius of the guy who invented the Bren gun but was later to learn that much better weapons had been invented. The German army's 88 mm was one.

The tedium of barrack life was shattered one day as we received a large contingent of men from the west coast. They were a different breed of cat from us prairie yokels. I don't think there was a farm boy in the lot. To begin with they had quite a sprinkling of Americans amongst them. Several of the Yanks had been soldiers of fortune who had fought in the recent war in Spain. In that war, which was a proving ground for all the new weaponry of Europe's dictators, the wrong side won. The Fascist General Franco, with the help of Hitler and Mussolini, managed to subdue the country and rule it with an iron fist until his death many years later. For reasons which still escape me the governments of the U.S. and Canada both frowned on their people fighting for the freedom of the people of Spain.

In the confines of barrack life the main entertainment for us green recruits was to sit on our bunks and listen to the newly arrived characters relate their many worldly experiences to us and to one another. Talk about a bunch of "rounders." Those guys collectively had been everywhere and done everything. Lumber jacks, hard rock miners, ex-cons, gamblers, hoboes, deep sea fishermen, con men, bigamists, no one you would invite into your home. But very interesting to listen to.

I recall that the winter of 1940-41 was long and hard. We had all been issued winter hats with ear lugs that could be pulled down and tied under one's chin. The quartermaster stores did not have anything in my size—7 and 3/4. That was unfortunate as I was the only one in my platoon who could not protect his ears from the extreme temperatures. The army, being run by some book that was written before the Boer War, did not give a lowly private soldier much leeway to discuss things like ear lugs with anyone in charge.

Shortly after we were issued those hats we had orders to "fall out" on parade in full battle order. It seemed that the C.O. had chosen the coldest night of the year to find out how effective gas masks would be in extreme cold. I think it was about thirty below zero F. In any event we were sent off on a route march wearing our gas masks, and I with my ears protruding. It was soon discovered that no one could see through their frosted up goggles and we returned to barracks. By that time both my ears were frozen solid.

I put in a very painful night and by morning both of my ears looked like balloons. I was afraid that I might even lose them. Every morning after breakfast the company commander came through our barrack room to inspect us. He wanted to see if we knew how to make our beds properly and shine the bottoms of our boots, and to spot check our rifles to see if they were properly cleaned and oiled and anything else his devious little mind could think of.

As I stood rigidly to attention at the foot of my bunk he looked me over and barked, "What the hell is wrong with your ears?" I explained to him that I had too many brains for the army as they didn't seem to have a winter hat in my size. He turned an even deeper purple than he had been able to obtain during his many years in the officer's mess and asked the sergeant to take my name. I could be in trouble.

Fortunately I had registered my condition with my platoon sergeant and was slated to go on "sick parade" to visit the Medical Officer. The M.O. took one look at my ears and, hearing the cause of their inflation, prescribed an inside job for me for the rest of the winter. He felt that my ears would be very susceptible to freezing again in which case I would be in danger of losing them. I was posted to the office of the Military District No. 10 Intelligence Officer. The hours were great as the I. O. spent as little time as possible in his office, as his friendly sergeant was to assure me.

It turned out that my sole duties as assistant to the assistant to the I. O. would be to peruse the three or four different newspapers which were delivered to the office every morning. In so doing I was to cut out with scissors any article appearing therein which could be closely related to anything military to do with the United States of America—even the contents of some speech by an obscure senator who discussed the way the war was going. These items were then handed to the sergeant, who I believe, then pasted them in some log that the I. O. would study if he felt he could spare the time from his hectic love life which was the envy of all.

Shortly after that posting, word came that some of the people who had mathematical ability and were able to read would be sent on a course near Kingston, Ontario, to learn regimental signals. I was selected for that course along with several others from my company. I still had the option of staying in the (Intelligence?) office but really couldn't see any future in that. It must have been the forerunner of all the bureaucratic jobs our government has learned to create.

I chose the signal course. Here again fate seemed to be on my side. I am sure that the knowledge of signals and map reading that I obtained on that course helped in no small way to qualify me for the job I actually was selected for in the FSSF a couple of years later.

Those of us chosen for the signals course were shortly on our way to Kingston, Ontario and the nearby camp Barriefield. The course was a pleasant diversion from the boring routines of barrack life in Fort Osborne. At least I once again had a chance to improve my mind by learning several skills requiring some study. The course was run by the Royal Canadian Corps of Signals and had some very fine instructors. We were taught the Morse Code, both the radio telegraph audio and the visual Aldus Lamp signals as used between ships at sea. I recall that we were required to read and send about twenty words per minute. The course also included map reading and map making and telegraph line maintenance and radio operation.

After the group I had come from Winnipeg with had been there about a month, our pay records had not yet caught up with us. As may be imagined we had no pocket money with which to buy the bare necessities such as cigarettes, beer, tooth paste and razor blades. Because of our "dire straits" the following episode presented an opportunity to create a "cash flow" in our group which could alleviate our poverty somewhat.

As we stood on parade for roll call the morning in question our Sergeant Major announced that the camp had no barber and asked for a volunteer to take the job. He painted a verbal picture of all the benefits which would befall the person who took the job. Those benefits included pocketing a fee of 15 cents per head from every customer; exclusion from such menial tasks as kitchen fatigue (pearl diving or bubble dancing), another name for dish washing; and exclusion from fire picket, a kind of night watchman patrol to make sure none of the huts burned down.

As he extolled the perks of the job he also mentioned that the canteen fund would buy all the equipment needed to set a barber up in business. The hours were not bad either, from just after supper until lights out around ten o'clock.

I was standing in one of the rear ranks when all of that was being explained and some of the jokers from my hut started the rumor that I was a barber. It gained strength up and down the line until one character shouted out "here." The Sgt. Major sent his orderly sergeant over to take the name of the volunteer. As he approached our area of the parade square the guys pointed at me and told him I was a barber in civil life. In the meantime they were all thinking that this was a chance to end the drought in our hut. They were thinking of the money I would earn that they may all share, at least until their pay books arrived. I went along with the deal as I figured anyone could cut hair good enough to suit the army, besides I had made up my mind that my buddies would be the ones I would practise on first. Little did I know at the time that the sergeant major would be my first customer.

About two days later I was called out of a lecture to meet with a barber equipment salesman from Toronto. I selected what I figured I would need to carry on in the business of barbering. The camp already had a barber's chair and the usual sink and mirror so the basic tools were all I needed. As the equipment I had ordered would take a couple of days to arrive from Toronto I had a couple of late afternoons to go into town and sit and watch barbers at work. I managed to satisfy myself that there was really not an awful lot to learn for my purposes.

It was a shock to find my first prospect was his royal highness the sergeant major himself. I had two things in my favour. He was an older WWI type who probably no longer cared what the ladies thought about his hair.

He also sported a rather stern looking brush cut which was almost army regulations at the time. I must have satisfied him as he gratefully handed over his fifteen cents, put his hat on and left me to serve customer number two.

Where were all those good buddies of mine who so badly needed a hair cut? It finally dawned on me that they were all broke and couldn't afford my services. There was by that time a long line-up of shaggy types who had been ordered to have a haircut before next parade. I think I dispensed with about ten or so that first evening. I was rapidly getting the hang of it. The next day in the mess hall during the noon meal I was sitting at one of the tables with some of my so-called "friends." They were watching the line of diners proceeding past to the serving tables for their chow. Every now and then one of my friends would point to a likely subject and loudly declare, "There's one." I tried to pretend I didn't know them.

I think that in the long run I had the last laugh. I became the banker for our hut and was able to loan some of those characters enough to tide them over until our pay records arrived a week or two later. One of my best friends, a "ladies man" from Swan River who was on the course with me, vowed he would never let me ruin his good looks. Before the course was finished, along with my barbering career, he swallowed his pride and sat in my chair and allowed me to give him one of the best haircuts he ever experienced in the army.

The course lasted three months and nicely took care of the winter for me. We arrived back in Winnipeg as spring was beginning. As I had done very well in the signal school I was posted to Specialty Company in Fort Osborne Barracks and was assigned to take further training in radio at a civilian trades school in downtown Winnipeg.

I became really interested in the workings of electricity and radio theory when our class advanced to another instructor who, though brilliant, had a voice with the oddest effect on me. I could not stay awake in his lectures. He admitted to me that others had experienced the same difficulty in some of his classes. We parted company amiably and I returned to being a regular infantryman with the rest of the foot sloggers.

The largest part of the summer of 1941 was spent doing drill and weapons training with many days spent out at the St. Charles ranges, just west of where the Assiniboia Downs Racetrack is now located. Firing on the range was a warlike experience as we got to really feel the heft and kick of high powered rifles and machine guns.

When we were not on the firing line we were working in the "butts" operating the large targets and marking the shots for those who were taking their turns at firing. It was a fairly dangerous job as the occasional round would strike the metal frame of a target mechanism or the concrete above our heads and ricochet around.

One day we got news that the Winnipeg Grenadiers had returned from doing garrison duty in Jamaica and were refitting to be sent to the Orient. They were asking for volunteers from our depot in Ft. Osborne. Most of us were just marking time until we could be sent to Britain to join our own regiment, the P.P.C.L.I., which had been in England since December of 1939. A lot of us were tired of waiting. I had pretty well made up my mind to apply to transfer into the Winnipeg Grenadiers and be shipped with that regiment to the exotic destination of Hong Kong.

As fate would have it I was catching a few winks on my bunk during lunch hour when my friend, Jimmy Jacobsen, a great guy from Winnipegosis, came by and shook me by the boot. He informed me that he had put my name, along with his, on a posted list which had just appeared on the bulletin board. The direction he had chosen for me was to the east instead of the west and Hong Kong. He insisted that we both transfer into the Regina Rifle

Regiment which was now in Debert Camp, Nova Scotia, and expected to leave shortly for Britain. I said "Thanks a lot, Jimmy. I was planning to go to Hong Kong." He told me to forget about Hong Kong, I was going to Britain with him. I said, "OK, Jimmy" and went back to sleep.

That was three months prior to Pearl Harbor and the Orient still looked pretty enticing. I probably owe my life to Jimmy as lots better men than I couldn't hack what the Japanese dished out to their prisoners for over three and a half years in their prison camps. Jimmy was killed in the Normandy landings on "D" Day.

Shortly after that we were bound on one of my life's greatest adventures. Because of wartime censorship it was advisable not to advertise troop movements. Because of the censorship I am sure that the enemy really knew a lot more about our movements and whereabouts than our next-of-kin ever did. After leaving Winnipeg every letter we wrote home was handed unsealed to our officers who had to read it and delete any reference to our plans or location. Wartime censorship was one of the restrictive measures we were to put up with as members of an active military unit. In retrospect I would also say that being in the Forces at the time was akin to being in prison physically and mentally in as much as we had lost our freedom to come and go as we wished. We also lost the choice of clothing, footwear, diet and even hair style. That was the aspect of wartime army life which has probably left its greatest imprint on my psyche.

The day we left Winnipeg was one which I shall always remember. The Union Station was crowded with many of the relatives and friends of those who were boarding the troop train which was to take us half way across Canada to Debert Station, Nova Scotia. In my case I had no one in particular in Winnipeg to see me off for which I was grateful. For many of my fellow travellers there were wives, sweethearts, very small children and a scattering of parents and siblings—a lot of very tearful goodbyes.

As I recall it our train had no Pullmans, at least for the "other ranks," as the majority of us were called. Consequently we journeyed all the way to Nova Scotia sitting in day coaches and catching what sleep we could in crowded and reasonably uncomfortable circumstances. I was later to learn that there were much more spartan modes of transportation in my adventuresome future.

Three or four days after our departure from Winnipeg our train pulled into a place named Debert Station just west of Truro, Nova Scotia. We were a grubby, unwashed lot as we gathered up our gear and filed off the train onto the platform. We had just managed to form up in a reasonable semblance of military order when a sergeant and a scruffy looking private came over to where we were lined up.

The private, who was one of the truck drivers, turned to the sergeant and said, "This looks like our bunch here, Bill." Coming from Fort Osborne Barracks we could scarcely believe our eyes and ears. A private calling a sergeant by his first name! That was the first impression we had of the kind of outfit we were casting our lot in with.

In all probability we would be going into battle with an undisciplined mob or the next thing to it. We hoped that what we had just witnessed was an isolated case or perhaps just some people from the motor pool who had been together too long.

As it turned out our apprehension about the lack of military discipline proved premature as the great majority of the men in the Regina Rifle Regiment were a different breed of cat from the parade square lot we had been indoctrinated with in Winnipeg. I believe we soon realised that we were then in a typical citizen army which would, in all likelihood, give the enemy a real run for his money when the chips were down. It became clear that corporals and sergeants in the "Reginas" earned their stripes by their ability to do what is best for the men under them and not by their ability to polish apples.

We were assimilated into the ranks of the "Reginas" without much fanfare. We were soon indistinguishable having been issued new shoulder flashes and hat badges. We also learned that in a rifle regiment we had black buttons on our wedge caps and privates were called riflemen. Our officers and NCOs were also distinguished by their black pips, crowns, and chevrons.

CHAPTER 3

Sea Voyage

L ittle time was spent at Debert as our date of departure was near at hand. For several days there was an almost frantic effort at housekeeping duties and packing of weapons, quartermaster stores, and records. Everything, it seemed, had to be wrapped in waterproof paper and sealed in large crates. The rationale for this escaped me as I figured that if our ship was torpedoed (as many were in those days), those heavy crates would be the last thing to be saved.

As our day of departure arrived we were marched to the station where we boarded another train for the two or three hour run to the wharves of Halifax. As our train pulled into a large wharf (Pier 21) we had glimpses of the ocean liner we were about to board. It seemed to be held together by many layers of dull grey paint, which was an unsuccessful attempt to cover its rust-streaked hull.

As so often happens during any military move from one place to another, alighting from the train we sat on our kit bags and waited, and waited, and waited some more. Our boredom was finally relieved as we watched in awe as a strange procession proceeded down the gangplank from the deck of our ship. They appeared to be some rather short Oriental types wearing sandals, loincloths, dirty T-shirts and turbans. They were all chained together and taken out of our sight by some military police. We never saw them again.

We were finally lined up to board our dubious looking transportation. As we stepped up to the gangplank we were each handed a mess card which designated which deck, compartment, and table we were allotted. We were also each handed a canvas bundle which turned out to be the hammock we would occupy for the voyage. At the top of the gangplank we were met by a military policeman who inspected our mess cards and directed us to the proper ladder (stairway) leading to our deck. In my case the deck I was to inhabit was "D" deck. "D" deck on that old "rust bucket" was four decks down from the open air promenade deck—one deck below the water line. No port holes. My card directed me to compartment number 6, and finally to table number 18. Fortunately I was able to find a couple of hooks on the ceiling above our table fairly close to the aisle. On those I hung my hammock. As the compartment filled with men the closeness of our quarters struck me with a passing shock of claustrophobia which I can too vividly recall in the telling.

There was an excitement which quickly overrode the discomforts of the day as we were launched on our great adventure. There is a lot to be said for youth. I was only nineteen years old. We were about to participate in an all too real game of "Russian Roulette," another name for crossing the U-Boat infested North Atlantic in the summer of 1941.

Hopefully the odds would be in our favour. Very few experiences in my lifetime have compared with the excitement, half-dread, half-anticipation, and the feeling of real adventure I had as I surveyed my new surroundings. Little did I know that before the war would end I was to walk the decks of at least fifteen ocean-going conveyances, some quite large and famous and some just large enough to qualify as ships.

In writing my memoirs I wanted to be sure of the name of the first ship I sailed on. I knew it to be either the Empress of Asia or the Empress of Russia. Knowing the name and address of one of the passengers I decided to write to him for clarification. He was good enough to have his secretary reply with the information I sought. He lives part time in Buckingham Palace.

From: Major The Hon. Andrew Wigram   **BUCKINGHAM PALACE.**

15th July, 1982

Dear Mr Cottingham,

     The Duke of Edinburgh has asked me to thank you for your letter.

     His Royal Highness was interested to hear about your time on the Empress of Russia. I am afraid, however, that this is not a matter with which His Royal Highness can assist, but I wonder if you have thought of contacting the Imperial War Museum. Their address is:-

     The Imperial War Museum,
     Lambeth Road,
     London SE1

Yours Sincerely

Andrew Wigram

At the time of the writing of my memoirs, I was unsure of the the name of the first ship that I sailed overseas on. I knew it to be either the Empress of Asia or the Empress of Russia. I took the liberty of writing to the only other passenger of same whose name and address I could be sure of. This letter from Buckingham Palace was in answer to my letter.

As it happened, our ship had just made a rather hectic run from Alexandria, Egypt, by way of the Mediterranean Sea and the North Atlantic to Boston and then to Halifax. Her main passengers included the remnants of the British garrison from the island of Crete. They had managed to escape to Egypt following the invasion of that island by German paratroops. Among the passengers was a young Royal Navy midshipman, Prince Philip of Greece. He is better known now as the Duke of Edinburgh. We encountered him often as we made our daily rounds of the promenade deck. Thus it was that he was the only person I could recall at this time who shared that voyage with me. My enquiry to him established the fact that it was indeed the Empress of Russia.

Having stowed our gear in D deck and having a chance to look around we climbed up to the promenade deck. We were curious as to the circumstances which prompted the arrest of the crew members we had witnessed being led away in chains. In conversation with various passengers who had just arrived from Egypt we learned that there was a minor mutiny in the stoke-hold of the engine rooms. Upon learning that the ship would be proceeding to Britain via Halifax after leaving Boston the stokers did not wish to be involved in any further wartime risks. They had experienced enough near misses by dive bombers in making their way through the Mediterranean. We also learned that in order for the ship to continue on its way to Halifax it was necessary for the captain to order a lot of his passengers into the stoke-hold and onto the business end of shovels. The Atlantic coast of North America was one of the prime hunting grounds for Hitler's undersea navy.

I cannot vouch for the fate of the poor wretches who were led away in chains but I can certainly describe the plight of their replacements who joined our ship in Halifax shortly before we sailed. I don't recall seeing them board the ship but when we were well out to sea with several hours sailing behind us we began to see young Canadian navy recruits coming out on deck for a breath of fresh air. They all had several things in common. They wore brand new uniforms and their most prominent features were their white teeth and the whites of their eyes. All of their exposed flesh was covered with black coal dust. Their hands had blisters which they could only hope would heal a bit before their next tour of duty in the stoke-hold. It was revealed that they were taken from the navy's manning depot in Dartmouth, across the harbour from Halifax. They had recently joined the navy "to see the world." Those who survived the war would never forget their rude introduction to ship-board life in the boiler rooms.

Our ship was one of six or seven liners and a few merchantmen (freighters) to form a convoy. We had several destroyers with us which continually sped back and forth around our perimeter searching for tell-tale signs or sounds of U-Boats. It was comforting to see such concern for our safety but there were no guarantees in those days. I had learned to read signal lamps during my course in Kingston so I found it quite interesting to watch the messages being flashed from ship to ship. In so doing I learned that the ship immediately on our starboard bow was the "Orbita" and was carrying the Royal Winnipeg Rifle Regiment.

With the exception of one very terrifying moment I cannot recall that voyage being anything but a great experience for this young prairie type. The incident in question happened one day when it was my turn to go down to the galley carrying a couple of buckets to collect the "swill" to feed the persons who shared table number 18 with me in our compartment.

I was lined up with about a hundred other bodies in a long passageway which led into the galley where the stew was being ladled out. We were really jammed tightly in that steamy corridor. So much for my claustrophobia. Just then we heard the loudest explosion that any of us had heard up to that date. Surely we had been torpedoed... In no time at all we would be resting in the vicinity of the Titanic. Strangely there was no panic in our crowded corridor, just baleful glances around to see who we were about to die with. The place did not appear to be flooding with cold sea water and the screws kept up their steady rhythm. Our apprehension gradually dissolved and we subsequently learned that the ship's crew had chosen that moment to limber up the five-inch naval gun which was mounted on the stern.

We were issued British money by our paymaster and had several days of journey left in which to acquaint ourselves with how to use it. One of our military police, who had been raised in Britain, kept a close watch on our transactions in the ship's canteen to make sure the "Brits" weren't cheating us. The North Atlantic was relatively calm for most of the trip but as we neared our destination we encountered some large swells. Sitting on the promenade deck and looking lengthwise fore and aft I was alarmed to note a considerable bending of the entire ship as it humped over a large swell or dropped into a deep trough. The wonder, to the uninitiated, was that at some point it did not break in two.

I recall that on our second last morning our convoy sailed through a lot of floating wreckage—very sad evidence of a sinking. On the first day of September we came up on deck to a very beautiful sight—the green hills of Scotland. We were steaming up the Clyde to Greenock. We had survived the "Russian Roulette" of an Atlantic crossing in the summer of 1941.

Welcome to Britain

After disembarking in Greenock we boarded a train. Its shrill piping whistle brought gales of laughter from all concerned. We were used to more masculine sounds from our train engines. The all-night train ride through the length of blacked out Britain was an exciting event. Evidence of the "Blitz" was a constant reminder that the war we had been training for was a reality indeed. The black-out was omnipresent and somewhat sinister. Occasionally we could see distant anti-aircraft tracer fire and the probing sweep of searchlights as they tried to pin point the odd enemy bomber. It was also novel to see almost everyone wearing steel helmets and carrying gas masks on the dimly lit platforms of the stations we passed through.

By the evening of our second day on the train we pulled into Aldershot station and were subsequently marched into what was known as Wellington barracks. I suppose it may have been built shortly after the Battle of Waterloo and was named to honour the winning general. The various living quarters would also serve well as prisons as the entire compound they were in was surrounded by a high brick wall, capped by broken glass embedded in cement. There was one exit from all that through a well guarded front gate which made Check Point Charlie look like the entrance to a playground.

Wellington Barracks was the only military abode I ever occupied in which, to my knowledge, I had to pay rent. We were advised that henceforth we would be charged sixpence per payday (a shilling per month) for barrack damages. We had come to Britain to help them protect the remnants of their Feudal System. The only way it seemed possible to damage their barracks would be with heavy artillery, of which we had none. Welcome to war-torn Britain.

I had my first leave in Britain at the home of my father's sister, Aunt Mabel Hume, in Sussex—not that far from Aldershot as the crow flies, but a half-day's travel by various antique trains and double decker buses. Aunt Mabel's husband was an officer in the Lifeguard Regiment. They were the ones who wore the white plumed helmets and silver breast plates as they rode beside the monarch's carriage on state occasions. He had served in the Great War but had retained his commission for some position in the Home Guard for World War II.

My next three months were spent in more infantry manoeuvres and parade square drill. We also became involved in defensive measures such as stringing barbed wire around critical targets such as the experimental air base at Farnborough. During that period we witnessed some weird and wonderful types of aircraft being test flown. We were occasionally inspected by various brigadiers and on one very special parade by King George the Sixth and his very popular spouse, the "Queen Mum."

After moving out of the Aldershot area we were posted to various country estates which had been commandeered by the War Department. One such posting was to a beautiful country spot which had been an exclusive golf and country club. Unfortunately no one bothered to inform some our our wilder types from the lumber camps and hard rock mines of Northern Saskatchewan that those smooth green places where the grass was so short were, in fact, golf greens. They were great places for making quick turns with bren gun carriers. I suspect the Canadian government had to pick up the tab for repairs to same as we were no longer being assessed barrack damages.

In early December 1941 I was issued a few days leave and again enjoyed the hospitality of the Humes in their beautiful home in Sussex. Once more they treated me like visiting royalty. It was there that we heard the news of the Japanese attack on Pearl Harbor. It seemed like only a week or two later that Britain was alive with American uniformed personnel. It became harder and harder to get a decent seat in a pub. The odd Yank was endearing himself to the Brits. When asked for two and six for the Scotch he had just ordered, he would reply, "How much is that in *real* money?"

On the 15th of December our regiment moved into a large estate a few miles south of Gatwick Airport. It was known as Hayward's Heath. While in that location we took part in many large manoeuvres with the whole Canadian Army. That included mostly marching in full battle order, with haversacks, gas capes rolled on top of same, our ancient Lee-Enfield rifles, water bottle on one hip and bayonet in scabbard on the other—all of the above attached to our heavy webbing cross straps and belt. The detested gas mask in its canvas pouch was ever present being firmly strapped to our chest between the two long pouches for bren gun ammunition magazines. We also carried ammunition pouches for our rifles. And worst of all were the W.W. I steel helmets we wore night and day.

Some days we marched as many as forty miles with a ten minute break every hour. I recall that on more than one occasion upon removing my boots to rest my feet I would find my socks stuck to my toes because of the congealed blood between them. Every night we were required to dig in (we also carried a folding shovel attached to our belt). After digging a slit trench large enough to give us personal cover in the event of an air raid we opened our haversacks and withdrew a rubberized ground sheet to cover ourselves with as we attempted to sleep in our mini-trenches. I am certain that in that manner we covered most of the southeast corner of England several times. I cannot recall that period of army life with any enthusiasm. Cold, tired, hungry, aching and wet says it all. Homesickness didn't count as that was one luxury we couldn't afford.

The seemingly never-ending misery of the cold and wet, and occasionally snowy, large scale manoeuvres were a constant fact of life. We were destined to endure far more route marching in such conditions than we felt would ever be required of us once we got into the real war. Europe was only so big and in all probability we would be unlikely to have to march more than a few miles of it in any given day.

Our living quarters, when we were privileged to occupy them, consisted of Quonset huts. They were large corrugated steel half culverts embedded in cement for their flooring. They were also known as Nissan huts. I can't believe the Brits bought them from the Japanese. The huts were heated by a very small stove centered mid way between the prefabricated wooden ends which contained our only doors and windows. They each held about thirty men.

To pass the evenings several card games entertained those of us who happened to have a few shillings to invest. The most popular game was high-low split poker. The stakes were never very high as a private soldier in those days was only paid a dollar and twenty cents a day and upon being posted overseas he had to sign over half of his pay to his next-of-kin for safe keeping. The net result was that he had the grand sum of twenty dollars a month with which to travel to London for a weekend every two or three months if he was lucky enough to survive the penny ante games of poker. I was fortunate at the time as I was promoted to corporal and received an extra twenty cents a day, half of which was assigned to my parents. Very few infantrymen came through the war with any love for Mackenzie King or the Liberal Party as a result of such largess.

I recall that during that miserable winter our coal supply was guarded at all times during the nights. Each hut was allotted a certain amount of coal which was probably determined in some manual for normal conditions. Our winter in Hayward's Heath was far from normal according to the natives who suffered along with us in Sussex that winter. It was the rule in our hut that anyone who had won more than a certain amount had to drop out of the game and make a one-man raid on the coal compound. The compound was surrounded by a single concertina, double apron, barbed wire enclosure which was tricky to get through unless you happened to know a very neat Commando tactic. As the corporal of our hut it was my lot to accompany the first guy who was detailed to steal coal and give him a few pointers as to how to get through the barbed wire. It was then up to him to pass on his expertise to the next guy who was so detailed.

That was best accomplished on a moonless night or one that was heavily overcast. It also helped if there was an air raid going on within twenty miles or so that might divert the attention of any guard. Anti-aircraft tracer bullets and searchlights always fascinated anyone who was far enough away to be out of danger. What a guy wouldn't do for a little comfort.

Mention of air raids may lead the reader to believe that poor old Britain was constantly under attack from the air. Such was the case before we arrived in the fall of 1941. The "Blitz", as the worst of the air raids were named, were a terrible time for most of Britain to live through. The East End of London took the worst pounding and had the most people killed and wounded. It was the closest large target to the bombers stationed in Germany and later from airfields in The Netherlands, Belgium and France. But other large cities were targets often enough that no one could relax for a good night's sleep. Manufacturing centres such as Sheffield, Manchester, Coventry, Liverpool and Nottingham, to name a few, also took quite a beating.

CHAPTER 5

Reprieve

re-prieve (ri-prev') n. 1, a temporary delay in the carrying out the sentence of a judge; 2, a temporary relief from pain or escape from danger;-v.t. { reprieved, repriev-ing}, 1, to grant a delay in the execution of; as, to reprieve a condemned prisoner; 2, to free for a time from pain or danger.

Events, beginning in June of 1942, were shaping up in such a way as to have a profound impact on the direction of my life forever after. Our regiment had moved from Hayward's Heath to Newhaven, a harbour town on the south coast. We began a different life entirely from that of seemingly endless route marches and simulated war manoeuvres. We were given the duty of helping to guard the country from invasion by way of the English Channel.

During that period I was selected by the brigade commander to help conduct a "battle school." The location of that endeavor was several miles inland among the downs of Sussex centered at a place called Lewes. The downs of southern England were misnamed as far as we were concerned. They should have been called the "ups." They were large rolling hills which had to be surmounted by us while heavily laden with all our equipment, which at times included a bren gun or an anti-tank rifle. The White Cliffs of Dover were composed of "downs" which had been eroded by the English Channel for centuries; solid chalk with a thin growth of vegetation on the top. It was great trying to sleep in a slit trench in the downs, especially in the rain. Our battle dress would be somewhat whitened by the chalk and water.

In helping to conduct the battle school, I, along with the other instructors were required to accompany every company in the brigade through a rigorous couple of days of forced marches through terrain very closely resembling battlefield conditions. We had to adopt a fairly mean mode in attempt at reality. If any of our instructees loved us we weren't doing our jobs properly. Instructing platoon commanders and NCO's in tactics which would serve them well under battle conditions was not my choice of a nice way to spend part of a summer. Some of our staff were involved in setting various traps for the advancing troops and using prepared charges to simulate artillery shells landing here and there and in some cases actually firing over their heads with live machine gun fire. It was all very realistic and exhausting to anyone who wasn't in top shape.

As there were basically nine companies in the three battalions which made up our brigade that meant it took us about three weeks to run every company through the course twice. During that period I became well acquainted with the brigadier and his staff, and he with me and the other NCO's who assisted in the course. When the course ended I returned to my unit which was still located in Newhaven. Upon my return I learned that the Canadian Army was asking for volunteers to form the nucleus of the First Canadian Parachute Battalion. I, along with about two hundred others from our regiment, hastily put our names on the list.

My mother used to say that idle hands can usually find mischief to do. I guess that is when my guiding fate, or whatever it is that makes some crucial decisions for us, had a hand in my future again. I use the word "again" as a couple of times prior to the event I wish to relate, my fate took a turn. Firstly, when I was refused immediate entry into the R.C.A.F. in Winnipeg. It was also working when my friend Jimmy Jacobsen volunteered my services to join the Regina Rifles rather than let me go to Hong Kong as I had planned.

I am not too proud of the kind of "mischief" my leisure led me into with the aid of a liquid substance better left in the keg.

On the evening in question I had some time off as a reward for the hectic three weeks that I had put in as an instructor at the battle school. It must have been the 18th of August, 1942. I found myself sitting in the public lounge of "The Ship', one of Newhaven's better pubs. I was having a rum or two or three with a couple of British sailors. I can't even recall their names but they seemed like a couple of real veterans with their tales of having this ship and that ship shot out from under them.

As the evening wore on they suggested that there were a few landing craft in our harbour which were about to depart on a "commando" raid. They also suggested that we three stalwarts should join them. Why not? I had just finished showing a bunch of troops what real action would feel like. Maybe it was time to put my money where my mouth was. We proceeded down to the docks and as my own platoon was on guard there that particular night we had no problem entering what was apparently a very restricted area. We proceeded up the ramp onto the first landing craft we came upon and were busily asking some of the troops on board if we could have some weapons to help them in their endeavour. It was strange to see a couple of battle tanks on a landing craft for commandos but I never gave it another thought. At that point a very disturbed officer came along and ordered us ashore. He followed us off the ship and hailed a couple of MP's and asked them to lock us up "for security purposes only" for the rest of the night. I was taken to our own regimental lock-up and given a bed.

First thing next morning we awoke to the news that it was no mere "commando" raid that we had tried to barge our way into. It was the trial run of a small scale invasion to be known for ever after as the "Dieppe Raid." I am not too proud of the part I almost played in it. What a horribly misplanned tactic it turned out to be. Many times since I have been humbled by the belief that the unknown officer who sent us ashore was some kind of guardian angel in disguise. I hope he survived the operation, whoever he was. A lot of good men didn't.

To add to the events of that historic night our regiment was being inspected the next morning by none other than "my friend" the brigadier. On making his rounds of our various establishments he had to poke his head into the lock-up. Upon seeing me he seemed just more than a little surprised. He blurted out, "What are you doing here Corporal Cottingham?" The regimental sergeant major who was accompanying him beat me to the punch by saying, "This man was found on board a landing craft about to depart for France last night, Sir!" The brigadier just shook his head and went on with his inspection of the rest of the room. I was released from the brig as no charges had been laid.

About a week later I was called to the orderly room and advised that I was the only one in the Regina Rifle Regiment to be selected for parachute training. The brigadier? No doubt! I felt that I had just won the Sweepstakes. I couldn't get into the air force but the paratroops had to be the next best thing. No more slugging it out with the infantry. I would ride into action in a plane. What an exciting prospect. How could a guy still be so dumb at the age of twenty? I was later to learn that after one's feet hit the ground he became an instant infantryman again. In no time at all I found myself on a train heading for a destination I had never heard of—a place named Ringway, up near Manchester. As the train proceeded north we were joined at almost every station by fellows from various units of the Canadian Army. By the time we changed trains in London for the long trip north we had quite a group, several of whom were to become lifelong friends. There were a total of eighty-five Canadians, mostly NCO's, and officers who were to be trained as paratroops by the R.A.F.

Without a doubt the parachute training at Ringway was the most exhilarating experience of my entire military career. The

R.A.F. instructors were tops. They did everything in their power to convince us that jumping from an aircraft was " a piece of cake." They were almost right. We spent the first week and a half learning how to exit from a hole in the floor of a Whitley bomber. They had a number of mock-up fuselages mounted about ten feet above some deep canvas mattresses. The object was to feed ourselves into the hole in the floor of these "planes'; alternating from fore and aft by sliding towards the hole in turn; swinging our feet into the hole and pushing off in such a manner as not to hit the previous jumper in the face with our steel clad army boots. A very tricky procedure to master. We also had to drop through a slightly tapered hole which was about four feet across and three feet deep with a parachute pack on our backs; land on the mattress and spring out of the way of the next jumper.

The large hangar we trained in also contained a number of parachute harnesses suspended from cables which allowed a long steep slide onto more mattresses. Using these we were taught how to control our descent and land without breaking a leg. The Brits had perfected a technique for landing safely which we were soon to learn was far superior to that which the Americans were still teaching. I believe that I am right in stating that we had about eighty-five men in our course who each made seven jumps without breaking a single leg.

While not practising exits and landings in the hangar we were occupied in a great deal of toughening up exercises which included forced marches. A forced march is comprised of alternately running a hundred yards and then briskly walking a couple of hundred yards. In doing that for several miles every day we must have lost a total of about eight hundred and fifty pounds among the lot of us in the two and a half weeks. Coupled with that kind of exercise we had to do a lot of push-ups and climb a thirty-foot rope suspended from the rafters of the hangar. I almost flunked out of the course on the latter as I have never been all that strong in the arms.

The evening before, we all had a chance to put our money where our mouths were so to speak. We were assembled in the hangar for a pep talk by the senior Canadian officer who was taking the course with us. He was an amiable chap from a famous Quebec regiment. He was quite in earnest as he explained to our gathering how important it was that each and every one of us must show these R.A.F. types what solid stuff we Canadians were made of. It was his honour to have been chosen the next morning to be the first Canadian soldier to make a military parachute jump.

What an historic moment we all looked forward to the next morning. Conditions in Tatton Park, our jump zone, were ideal as we strapped on our parachutes in anticipation and above all, in hopes that we would have what it takes when the instructor gave us a "Go." At the windward edge of the field there were two huge barrage balloons tethered to trucks. The trucks had winches for raising them and bringing them back to earth. An instructor and our senior officer along with three other men were loaded into the basket which hung from cables beneath the first balloon. There was just room enough in the basket for an instructor to stand in one corner and for four men to sit along each side on the floor. Each of the men were required to attach the static line from their parachute pack to a cross-bar which formed a squared arch over top of the basket. After the balloon was allowed to float up to a height of 750 feet the winch was braked to hold it steady. The little wind that there was kept it at a safe angle from the cable leading down to the truck.

Everything was in readiness for the the great moment for which we had all been trained. The instructor yelled, "Action stations number one." At which point the first jumper was to swing his feet into the exit hole and prepare to shove himself off and drop through the hole. From the ground we heard the instructor yell, "Go." The very next thing we heard was a loud plaintive cry. We were stunned. No one dropped through the aperture on command. There was a hasty conference among the instructors on the ground who were in telephone communication with the instructor in the balloon. Shortly the balloon was hauled down and a distraught major was led away to a staff car. We never saw him again.

Following the two balloon jumps we each managed to do that day our week proceeded without undue incidents. It is worth noting that when sitting in a balloon's basket seven hundred and fifty feet above the ground it is almost spooky how quiet things become. None of the earthly sounds we take for granted can be heard up there. We were able to hear our hearts beating in the stillness. Our instructors were pretty cool—they didn't have to jump but I know they must have had their share of same to become instructors. As each jumper exited the basket it was the duty of the instructor to gather in the empty canvas bag which now hung at the end of the previous jumper's static line. Invariably he would comment upon looking down the hole, "His opened." Most reassuring!

To complete the course we were required to do five drops from an aircraft. At that stage the only planes available for our training were the ancient Whitley bombers. They were just a little more advanced than those used in World War I. They were only large enough to hold eight jumpers and one instructor in the cabin. They were twin-engined machines with a nose which appeared to droop. Not very handsome vehicles but I guess they couldn't spare anything newer with the demands of the war at the time. We were rushed for time as we had already been booked to sail for North America to join up with the first Canadian Parachute Battalion in Fort Benning, Georgia. Thus it was that to complete our seventh and final jump they took us up in less than ideal wind conditions and dropped us from a mere five hundred feet in the dark of night. To the best of my knowledge we all survived that drop without major injuries.

The final day at Ringway was short as we had a "wings" parade in the morning during which we became the first Canadians to wear the blue and white parachute wings of the British Army. Those were worn on the right shoulder just above chevrons if you happened to be an NCO. We were issued rail passes to return to our various regiments for final documentation prior to embarking for the voyage back to North America.

Upon returning to The Regina Rifle Regiment I felt like the conquering hero as my friends gathered around to ask all about the parachute training and wish me bon voyage. A lot of those fine fellows, many of whom I would never see again, would go on to make their mark on "D" Day and the horrible battles through the hedgerows of Normandy.

I was submitted to an extensive medical examination. That was followed by documentation from battalion headquarters and a welcome conference with the paymaster. I was then issued a rail pass to Greenock, Scotland. I was to sail out from the same port at which I entered the country about one year earlier. Imagine my surprise as our train pulled into the docks of Greenock, and there, a couple of miles off shore, was the most famous liner of all waiting for us to board. The Queen Mary.

CHAPTER 6

The Queen Mary

F or anyone unfamiliar with ships it was a real eye opener to sail out into the Clyde on a harbour ferry and come alongside the "Mary." As we approached her it was difficult to believe that anything that large could attain speeds of forty knots in the open ocean. Boarding that marvelous ship was like going to the circus when we were kids. There was an air of expectation unlike anything I had experienced before as we made our way to the stateroom we were to share for the voyage.

Our quarters were on "B" deck, only two decks below the Promenade deck, which, on the "Mary" was only one deck below the Boat deck. Seventeen of us shared quarters originally meant for two persons but compared to the hammocks on "D" deck on the old Empress of Russia it seemed like heaven. We had three-tiered bunks which were installed to convert the "Mary" into a troop ship. Fully loaded she carried about eighteen thousand troops. On our trip there were only about two thousand souls on board.

Besides the relative luxury of our stateroom there was the most fantastic main dining room for our meals. It had the dimensions of a large concert hall and at one end was a mural depicting the Atlantic Ocean. A light which moved from Greenock towards New York indicated our progress from day to day. But best of all was the food. White bread and butter were things we hadn't seen since we left Canada and we could "pig out" on those two items to our heart's desire.

The "Mary" was so large and so fast that it required no escort but relied on coded messages from the Admiralty to zig-zag its way across the Atlantic, hopefully avoiding any known U-Boat locations. Intercepted messages revealed that Hitler had offered a reward of one hundred thousand dollars to any U-Boat captain who could sink her or her sister ship the Queen Elizabeth. About our third day out we heard what sounded like a war going on above our heads so we rushed up on deck to see what was happening. Unknown to us the whole top deck was equipped with anti-aircraft guns of various calibres, including the mighty Bofors rapid fire cannons. They were launching small balloons and firing at them. We were most impressed with the amount of armament and the deafening roar of its use. Fortunately it was just practice as there were no aircraft in sight.

The route we were allotted by the Admiralty took us far south of the regular shipping lanes. The last night of our voyage it became so hot and humid in our stateroom that I and several others took a pillow and a blanket up to the open deck at the ship's stern to try sleeping in the open air. It proved to be a more comfortable location and we had no trouble falling into a deep sleep. Several hours later I was certain that we had been torpedoed and were sinking fast. I awoke with a start as water was flowing over my face with such force as to give that impression. It turned out that we had sailed into a tropical downpour of very warm rain which came in such quantities that it couldn't spill off the deck fast enough and formed a large pool which began to slosh back and forth with the gentle rolling of the ship. That was the second time I was sure that I was about to enter Davy Jones Locker."

The next morning we were all on the lookout for the first signs of land in the west. We had been at sea for over five days on one of the fastest ships in the world and even though we had been zig-zagging quite a bit we knew we were getting close to land. It is actually possible to smell land and all its pollutants while still quite some distance from it. To verify our nearness to land we were joined shortly by a U. S. Navy blimp which came out to meet us and scout for signs of any U-Boats which may have been lying in wait for traffic in and out of New York. The blimp was similar to the ones used today to advertise Goodyear tires at football games, golf matches and auto races.

We were met by two destroyers which were detailed as escorts to bring us into New York Harbour. The entrance to such a busy port was considered a prime hunting ground for enemy submarines. As we approached the coast we could see the towers of Manhattan rising on the misty horizon and it was then that our destroyers began an impressive show. They began to put on a burst of speed and manoeuvre about throwing off depth charges. It was an awesome display as the explosions of the charges sent water towering about a hundred feet into the air. Whether they had targets under the sea or not we would never know but it was really something to see.

Eventually we sailed past the Statue of Liberty and into the harbour where we were met by several fire boats which shot streams of water hundreds of feet into the air with their equipment. Many small craft came out to meet us and sounded their whistles and horns. I shall never forget the gut shaking vibrations of the first notes of the Queen Mary's answering fog horn. What a deep bass voice the old girl had.

We soon learned that the port of New York was experiencing a tug boat strike. First indication of that was that the "Mary" had slowed to an almost imperceptible pace in navigating towards her berth far up the Hudson River. At this point our eyes had taken in so much of the New York skyline that it was almost overpowering to the senses after five and half days of seeing nothing but the flat Atlantic. As we approached our pier we sailed past what was known as "Liner Row" where the largest ships afloat were berthed. As we passed the huge Queen Elizabeth, the largest ship in the world, we could see the stricken Normandie as she lay on her side in the adjoining berth. Her three beautiful funnels were almost touching the water. She had burned in her berth several months prior to our arrival and presented a sickening picture. If it were possible to mourn the loss of an inanimate object everyone who saw that scene felt pangs of sadness.

About one year later, as we passed through New York on our way to Newport News, Virginia, we saw the rusted hulk of the Normandie being towed down the Hudson River towards Brooklyn where she was sold by auction and cut up for scrap. It had been by far the most beautiful ship ever built.

Arriving at center river opposite our intended wharf, which was right next to the stricken Normandie, our captain proceeded to berth the "Mary" without the use of tug boats. Fortunately there was little or no wind that day. Had there been he would have had to anchor in center stream and we would have had to disembark onto a ferry boat for transfer to shore. As it was, he demonstrated expert seamanship. Using only his rudders and screws (propellers) he inched the great ship into her berth. He did it so carefully that it was difficult to discern any movement for several hours. During all the while we had a "ring-side" view of the Normandie from our starboard rail.

In September of 1942 the New York Harbour Authority was still of the opinion that the burning of the Normandie had been an act of enemy sabotage. She had been undergoing conversion as a troop transport. Consequently before we were permitted to disembark we counted almost one thousand military policemen boarding our ship. They were finally stationed throughout the ship in such a manner as to be able to see down every passageway. Any spy who wanted to sabotage the "Mary" would have had to swim under her and plant a bomb.

After a very long day, most of it spent docking without the assistance of tug boats, we disembarked and were taken across the harbour on a ferry and entrained for the trip to Canada and home.

CHAPTER 7

The "Force"

A fter a brief leave spent with my parents in Swan River, I and the others who trained with me in England, were shipped to Fort Benning, Georgia, for training in the American parachute school located there. In 1942 Ft. Benning contained as many soldiers as there were people in the city of Winnipeg, about two hundred and fifty thousand. The methods of parachute training in the American Army were as different as night is to day from the friendly and supportive measures used by the R.A.F.

The instructors at Benning did everything in their power to try to convince us that jumping from an aircraft was going to be the most difficult and dangerous thing we were ever most likely to accomplish. The course consisted of several weeks of very physical exercises which included long runs in the Georgia heat, many push-ups, unarmed combat (ju-jit-su) and climbing a thirty-foot rope suspended from the rafters in a hangar. Included in that regimen were very tedious instructions in the packing of parachutes. It was required for each participant to pack his own parachute prior to each jump. That was incentive enough to pay attention in the lectures.

We soon learned that in two critical areas the Americans were sadly lacking in technique and equipment. They were teaching jumpers to land with their feet apart at shoulder width and perform a forward acrobatic tumble upon contact with the earth. That procedure resulted in at least one broken leg from almost every "stick" of fourteen jumpers who landed. In Britain we were taught to land with our feet and knees tightly together and crumple our bodies into the ground, feet, knees and shoulders, in that order in a sideways manner. To the best of my knowledge eighty-five of us did a total of seven jumps apiece without a serious injury in Britain.

The other area in which they were still in the dark ages was in their parachute harness and the deployment of the silk from the back-pack upon exit from a plane. In both countries the parachutes were deployed by a static line which was attached to the interior of the plane to pull the chute out of the pack as the jumper fell away. In Britain the jumper fell the distance of the shroud lines which then pulled the silk out of the bag allowing it to open without a great snap. In the American system the static line pulled the silk out first allowing the prop blast of the engine ahead to snap the silk into full bloom and the jumper to experience an almost whiplash or broken skull as the lines and their metal connectors shot passed his head.

We had a quick-release junction box on the center of our chest into which all of the webbing straps fitted and could be released by merely twisting the cover a half-turn and banging it with a fist. The American harness was very uncomfortable and was held in place tightly by a series of heavy snap fasteners which were originally designed for the harness of draft horses. I would estimate that it took about four or five times as long to get out of as that of the Brits. On the plus side for the Yanks I would like to say that they did have a reserve chute in case the main canopy did not open. Most of us figured that it was to satisfy the folks back home that parachuting was safe. In all of the many parachute jumps I have witnessed I must admit to seeing one chute failure in which the jumper used his reserve just in time to merely break a leg.

Towards the end of our training in Georgia we were visited by an officer from a secret unit known as the First Special Service Force. He was allowed several hours to try to sell us on joining his unit, which at the time was training for a special mission at a camp in the foothills of the American Rockies. He must have been a good salesman because he persuaded seventeen of us to join him for his trip west to Montana.

Our introduction to the "Force", as it became known to all of its members, was a frightening, and at the same time, exhilarating experience. We soon learned that it was no ordinary run-of-the-mill unit. There were unsettling signs that we may have committed ourselves to the possibility of a suicide mission or the next thing to it. I can't recall that any of us were persuaded to change our minds about the prospects of being part of such an enterprise. A lot of situations were fraught with danger in those days.

First off we were issued American Army clothing which was "space age" compared to the "King's Burlap" we had all worn in the Canadian Army. The "walking out" uniform was a very dapper outfit which even included neckties. We were issued a distinctive lanyard made from braided nylon parachute cords dyed red, white and blue. That item was worn through the epaulet of the left shoulder and buttoned under the flap of the left jacket pocket. Our field service caps were natty looking wedge caps which fit snugly and and had red, white and blue piping around them. The brass buttons on our tunics required no polishing and our fine trouser legs were worn tucked into highly practical parachute boots. The boots were a distinctive mark of the paratrooper and were not issued to any other branch of the services. We were also issued combat clothing which included special paratroop pants with large pockets. It was difficult to anticipate when you would meet with follow-up food, shelter or medical supplies after dropping into enemy held territory. Steel helmets issued to us were like football helmets with chin straps that had a special cup for the chin to fit in.

As winter came early in the Rockies we were issued white parkas and ski pants, very expensive mitts and ski boots. We were also issued skis and ski poles. The ski harness was the primitive bear trap type which was o.k. for straight cross country skiing but could prove very damaging to ankles and leg bones in any tumble on a downhill slope. I was one of the lucky ones who managed to survive several bad spills in the ski training which ensued and still ski away under my own steam. Many didn't. Our base hospital had many more ski casualties to deal with than those from parachuting accidents.

The weapons we were issued were all developed in the twentieth century unlike the old Lee-Enfield rifle I had carried in the Canadian Army. We were armed with M1 Garand .30 calibre rifles which were semi-automatic and held a clip of eight bullets. It was an ideal combat weapon. All one had to do to fire it was to work the bolt to put the first round into the chamber and then squeeze the trigger. When the eighth round was fired the empty clip went flying into the air leaving the action open for you to insert the next clip with one swift movement. I managed to qualify as an expert on that weapon. At platoon level we also had several Browning .30 Calibre belt fed machine guns—one for each section. Section leaders were issued Thompson sub-machine guns in lieu of the Garand rifle. They fired .45 cal. rimless ammunition which also fit the .45 Colt semi-automatic pistol we were all issued. The latter were worn in a quick-draw holster which hung from our web belts and was strapped to our leg with a rawhide thong. We also were issued a special combat knife which was designed expressly for our unit. It has since become a collector's item with a ridiculous value. It was such a mean little weapon that I foolishly threw mine overboard as we left our last combat area.

Our group from Fort Benning was housed together for the purpose of giving us a crash course in the weapons we had been issued. We were also brought up to date on American drill and military courtesies, Tables of Organization, (War Establishment) and other terminologies pertaining to America's way of doing business. I was no longer an "other rank" but an "enlisted man." I enjoyed the newness of everything to which we were exposed.

Our training began in earnest. We were expected to master several techniques which were to be used in carrying out what appeared to be a very dangerous mission. To satisfy the commanding officer that we had sufficient parachute training we were required to do two jumps from a C47 (Dakota) aircraft. Unlike Fort

Benning we did not have to pack our own parachutes. The "Force" had its own parachute rigger section which looked after that tedious procedure for the combat echelon as the three combat regiments were called. The rigger section was part of the service battalion of the Force which was a separate entity from the combat people and relieved us of all the mundane chores such as cooking and dish-washing, laundry, guard duty, truck driving, parachute packing and supply and armament maintenance. In action they were subject to some of the same dangers as the combat echelon even though they were mostly behind the lines. Our base medical people were in ser-vice battalion and many of our litter bearers were wounded or killed as were some of the supply people and truck drivers.

Regarding the two jumps we were required to do to satisfy the "Force" an incident worthy of note happened during the first of our two jumps. One of the men who came from Britain with our group was a full blooded Canadian Native by the name of Tommy Prince. He was a fine athlete and was quite proud of his accomplishments with the Canadian Army in Britain. He had been an outstanding runner and boxer, having won honours in both of those events dur-ing Division Games.

As we all became airborne in our trusty "Dakota" to do our first jump we were a fairly confident lot. Old hands—we thought. There was the usual friendly banter and show of bravado. As we stood up and hooked up our static lines prior to exiting the aircraft we were each required to visually check the equipment of the fellow ahead of us. The fellow behind me patted my "chute" pack and suggest-ed that it appeared to be full of old laundry. That was a sample of the nonchalance our group had developed towards our training. We considered ourselves pretty smart apples. There were fourteen of us in the aircraft and as we exited and our chutes opened we looked around to make sure everyone's chutes had opened. In that case we counted only thirteen chutes. After landing and rolling up our chutes we gathered together and tried to ascertain who was missing. Someone said, "Where's Tonto?" our nick name for Tommy. At that point we observed the aircraft making a circuit of the jump zone again. As we watched one lone parachutist came out and descended into our midst. We gathered around him and his first words were, "I guess I'm a chicken Indian." He apparently had a bad moment as he stepped to the door of the plane but was able to convince the jumpmaster to give him another chance. Normally anyone refusing to jump was whistled off to the Canadian Army as being unable to cut it with the F.S.S.F. In Tommy's case it was just as well he was given another chance as he went on to become one of the most decorated men in the outfit. Years later, in the company of Ex-Forcemen Allan Lennox and Hughie McVeigh, I was able to attend the unveiling of a bronze bust of Sergeant Tommy Prince in Kildonan Park in Winnipeg. The ceremony was also attended by Winnipeg's Mayor, William Norrie, Senator Guildas Molgat, and some Princess Pats who were his comrades in the Korean War.

Besides qualifying as parachutists again we were required to become proficient in mountain climbing; map reading; cross country skiing; the use of high explosives for demolition purposes; unarmed combat; and general survival under the most difficult conditions. We were provided with special over-snow vehicles which were manufactured by the Studebaker Corporation. They were known as "Weasels." They were designed to be dropped by parachute to assist us in the dangerous mission for which we were training. They carried a driver and one passenger seated in tandem like a small aircraft.

The weasel was capable of travelling about fifty miles per hour over the snow even while towing a half dozen of us on skis with our back packs and rifles. As luck would have it we never had to find out how efficient they would be in an actual operation. (That's another story.) They still had a lot of bugs to iron out when last I drove one.

When the "weasels" were not in use they were stored in the same building that housed our parachute rigging tables and drying towers. One very cold night there was a fire alarm which woke the entire camp and we discovered that the building with the "weasels" in it was on fire. The first of us to reach the building decided that we could drive some of the weasels out before the fire reached that end of the shed. I believe we got most of them out before things became too hot to handle. Fortunately for some of the characters who managed to drive them too far that night there was a blizzard blowing which covered their tracks. We learned by the grapevine that several of them ended up on nearby ranches and were used by "friends" for deer hunting.

Our ski training was carried out under very rigorous conditions. We were trucked up into a railway pass in the Rockies and given our first "opportunity" to use our winter equipment. It was all considered "state of the art" at the time. We had sleeping bags which rolled up into a ball about one foot in diameter. They were insulated with eider down and when zippered up we were quite comfortable in them even at forty below. We were housed in railway boxcars on a siding in a whistle stop by the name of "Blossberg." The name may have been supplied by one of our Norwegian ski instructors who was homesick. I recall that other than the string of boxcars on the siding there was no other sign of habitation in the area.

We spent a week up in that mountain pass. It was actually the Great Divide where all of the rivers flowing west from there ended up in the Pacific and all flowing east ended up in the Gulf of Mexico. There was no heat in any of the "bunk" cars. After several nights the uninsulated walls of our sleeping area were covered with a buildup of ice like the interior of a freezer. We were awakened each morning by one of the cooks in the heated "cook car" banging on a steel triangle which hung outside his door. Dressing for the day's exercises was a speedy affair to say the least. Breakfast and supper were always great meals. They were eaten in the relative comfort of the "cook car." We carried haversack lunches with us for the many miles we put in during the days. When it came time to eat them we usually built a fire to thaw out the sand-wiches. Our days consisted of trekking up many hills and practis-ing snow plow turns, telemarks, and stem christies.

We became reasonably proficient at controlling our skis in downhill situations. Those who couldn't were long gone. For any-one unlucky enough to break a bone during the training we had a couple of weasels available as makeshift ambulances. As our group was strictly Canadians the Norwegian instructors were astounded at the few casualties we had. Most of us had skied as kids unlike many of the Americans who had trained before us. Many of the fel-lows from the South had never seen snow prior to coming to Montana. At the completion of the ski course we skied out of the mountain pass down to a highway where we were met by trucks to take us back to Ft. Harrison.

During all of the training the Force went through there was a con-stant weeding out of those who didn't measure up. It was estimated that the Force went through twice as many men as they finally kept. We spent a lot of time in lectures after hours. Subjects such as demo-litions and mountain climbing were new to all of us and we had some excellent instructors in those fields. One such instructor was Lincoln Washburn of National Geographic mountaineering fame.

The next two weeks were spent in mountain climbing and demolitions training. In mountain climbing we learned how to use ice axes, pitons, various ropes and slings and became proficient at rappelling down the face of cliffs on a single line. We had to be able to do the latter with a "wounded" man supported on our chests. Strangely it was easier to do than it appeared at first glance. The "hairy" part of mountain climbing was in scaling almost vertical rock faces relying on driving pitons into cracks with a hammer. We were required to be roped to a couple of other men before any move upward in that manner.

I found the demolition training to be quite impressive. Our Force was the first to use a concentrated explosive called Ryan

Special. It was invented by our instructor, a Captain Ryan. RS, as it was shortened to, was three or four times as powerful as TNT and was particularly effective against steel and concrete. It was also used in conjunction with Primacord. Primacord was used for connecting charges which were placed at some distances from each other. It resembled a fuse in appearance but was actually filled with TNT enabling instantaneous explosion of all charges so connected. The two combined to be very effective for use in sabotage. I only had one occasion to use my demolition skills as I will attempt to relate in another chapter.

By that time it was fairly common knowledge, to us at least, that we were being trained for a very dangerous mission indeed. The target of our endeavors was a hydro-electric plant in Norway. Allied Intelligence was almost certain that the occupying German forces there were using that facility to power their experiments in the production of heavy water. Atomic and hydrogen bombs were unheard of in 1942 except for the very secretive scientists who were working to perfect them. With efforts to produce heavy water the enemy was certainly on the right track. It was later proved to be one of the ingredients in the manufacture of the more powerful hydrogen bomb.

Shortly after learning of our proposed mission we received news that it was cancelled as the Norwegian government (in exile in London) decided that destroying their national power source would be harder on their people than it would be on the enemy. If it were possible to hear a collective sigh of relief from about twenty-five hundred men—maybe God heard it. Shortly after that our training was altered somewhat to justify our designation as special shock troops and plan for more infantry-like missions.

Our group had been working overtime to catch up with the training the Force had received prior to our arrival. When it was time for Christmas leave most of the seasoned personnel who had completed their training were allowed off for a week or two. No such luck for our group as the commanding officer still looked upon us a "rookies." He didn't take into consideration that those of us who had been overseas for some time had far more training in battle drill and commando tactics than his beloved Force had in their past six months or so.

As a result, a group of us—seventeen to be exact— took it upon ourselves to take some unauthorized leave and to hell with the consequences. After several clandestine meetings we arranged to take a bus to Lethbridge, Alberta and trains from there to our various homes in Canada. There must have been a leak in our security because when our bus stopped at the bus station in Shelby, Montana, a couple of guys who looked like ranchers got on board. They began to direct the bus driver to a certain location in the town. One of them turned and faced us and opened his sheep skin jacket to reveal a metal star pinned on his shirt. He announced that he was the Sheriff of Shelby and that the gentleman with him was his Deputy. His next words were, "All you soldier boys are under arrest."

The bus pulled up in front of a formidable looking building with bars on the windows. We were herded inside and documented as guests in the local "Crow Bar Hotel." We were each given a blanket and marched upstairs and into a cage made of woven flat steel bars. It held the seventeen of us with plenty of room to spare. One of the blankets we had been issued was immediately put to good use and spread on the floor as someone produced a set of dice. "Galloping Dominoes" was an American army pastime that we had adopted over the past month or so.

Our dice game was interrupted by the sheriff who was all smiles as he came up with an unusual proposition. Apparently the war had taken most of the eligible young men from the town of Shelby and the sheriff's daughter and her friends heard about the busload of paratroopers her father had "on ice." They talked him into sending us, under guard of course, down the street to one of the local bistros which had a small dance floor and a juke box. We were happy to oblige the young ladies and spent several happy hours in their company as they fed the Wurlitzer nickels and bought us the odd drink. At closing time we were all herded back to the "Bastille."

The next morning an officer arrived with army transport and escorted us back to Fort Harrison and into the Force stockade. There we awaited our trial as we were all charged with being absent without leave. Our trials the next day were hasty and relatively painless. While waiting my turn to be called up in front of the senior Canadian officer, whose office was across the road from the building in which we waited, I was discussing the training weaknesses of the hot-shot outfit we had recently joined. It is well that I must have made a few points. Unknown to me the commander of second battalion, first regiment (then a major) Jack Akehurst, was sitting in the same room behind a large pot-bellied mountain stove. It took up a lot of space in the centre of the headquarters hut. He had heard every word that was discussed.

When I had finished "sounding off" he came out from behind the stove and beckoned for me to come over and talk with him. I thought I was really in trouble then for certain. He was a real gentleman and sincerely wanted to discuss a lot of things pertaining to the training of his battalion. I think he was impressed with my coverage of some of the courses I had in commando tactics in Britain. In any event it came my turn to "face the music" across the street in the mini court-marshall. I was subsequently reduced to the rank of private and sent back to my quarters.

Of the seventeen of us who were together in Shelby jail three of them did not make it through the war. They were R. C. Ashley of Windsor, Ontario, W. B. (Bill) Harry of Prince Albert, Saskatchewan, and Bill Brotherton of Medicine Hat, Alberta. Several were dropped from the Force rolls prior to going into action.

Three of them have been life long friends: Spud Wright of Grande Prairie, Alberta; Gerry Rusconi of Regina Beach, Saskatchewan; and Herb Peppard of Truro, Nova Scotia. Spud

Wright was one of the most decorated men in the Force. He was promoted to officer rank in Italy and critically wounded in southern France. Rusconi was also wounded in southern France, shot through the hand while reaching up to pick a cluster of grapes as he crawled forward towards an enemy position*. Herb Peppard was wounded in the final days of the Italian campaign and joined up with us again in southern France. He actually left his hospital without leave to be back with his unit. After receiving a formal dressing down by Colonel Akehurst for being AWOL, the colonel broke into smiles and awarded him the American Silver Star for saving one of his men under extreme conditions in the Italian campaign. I can't imagine a more select company than the one I shared in the Shelby jail.

*Rusconi tells a wonderful story about this incident that is worth repeating here. He and the German who shot him ended up in the same hospital room together; one of our guys wounded the German right after Rusconi was wounded. According to Gerry, the German had been a bellman at the Waldorf Astoria in New York City before the war, and spoke good English. "He was a nice guy," says Rusconi. "We had a good time together."

CHAPTER 8

Promotion

Having been demoted to the lowest form of life in the army on the 29th of January, 1943 it came as quite a surprise when Major Akehurst called me into his office on the 12th of March. I wondered what I had done. Had I broken another army rule? Our meeting that morning turned out to be very satisfying. My battalion commander had been reading my records and noted the various courses I had been on. He was apparently impressed with my qualifications and suggested I try out as battalion operations sergeant.

The posting would make me a key member of his headquarter staff. I was to be in charge of the headquarter NCO's, mostly sergeants and American T4's. In the American army a T4 wore three stripes with a T under them which was a technical rank paying the same as a sergeant but without the authority of a sergeant. They were people who had been on courses in reconnaissance, signals, intelligence and supply. We also had some privates who were trained as medics and one fellow who spoke German who was expected to interrogate any prisoners we might take. My own expertise was in commando tactics, map reading, map making and morse code (both audio and visual).

Major Akehurst outlined my duties, which included a very close liaison with himself and the battalion second in command, a Captain Sulo V. Ojala. I assured him I would make every effort to live up to his expectations. He then handed me a set of staff sergeant stripes. I somehow managed to perform satisfactorily in the job as I held that position for the duration of my days in the Force. Major Akehurst went on to become a colonel and commander of the First Regiment and Ojala was promoted to major prior to our first posting overseas.

Jack Akehurst was an ideal leader for such a select unit. He had been a mining engineer at Kirkland Lake, Ontario, in civil life. He entered his military career as an officer in the Lake Superior Regiment when the war broke out but hastened to transfer into the Force when that opportunity arose.

Sulo V. Ojala was an exceptional character. He had played hockey for the Chicago Black Hawks in his early twenties. Although an American he was familiar with Manitoba as he used to accompany Clark Gable on duck hunting trips to the Delta Marshes north of Portage la Prairie. Ojala was a crack shot with a pistol and a rifle. He had served with the Alaska Scouts for several years and later the Federal Bureau of Investigation. He was on loan to the Force from the FBI. Sadly, he became the very first in our headquarters to be killed in action in Italy.

Being in Battalion H.Q. we shared the same office as the first Battalion H.Q. and first Regiment H.Q. There were two battalions in each of the three combat regiments of the Force. Our regimental commander was a West Point graduate, Colonel Alfred Cook Marshall. He was affectionately referred to as "Cookie" behind his back. He happened to be a nephew of General George C. Marshall, later the instigator of the world famous "Marshall Plan." Over the next two years I was to get to know the personnel of the three headquarters on a more personal basis than those of the line companies.

Adding to the almost continual "high" we were on by being part of that unique unit was the ambience of the rocky mountain city of Helena. It still had the frontier flavor of its gold rush days. The main street was called "Last Chance Gulch." It was a great place to unwind after a week of intensive and sometimes dangerous training. The neon-lit saloons and free spending Americans we were rubbing shoulders with made every trip into town an exciting experience. The city of Helena endeared itself to the Force to the extent that it has been like a second home to many of us these past fifty years or so.

Shortly after my promotion to Staff Sergeant I was finally given a pass to travel home to Swan River. The only way to travel in those days was by train. I really enjoyed train rides even though they were much slower than today's methods of travel. I had to use several different railways to reach my destination. The Great Northern took me to Minot, North Dakota where I transferred to the Soo Line which took me to Moose Jaw, Saskatchewan. As our train stopped at the Canadian border I got off and was walking down the platform for some exercise. I was standing admiring the engine, a monster coal burning steamer. The engineer poked his head out of his window and asked me if I would like to make the rest of my journey in the cab with him and the fireman. I jumped at the chance as I had longed for such an opportunity ever since I was a small boy. I guess a guy like me never really grows up!

Before long the train moved out and quickly attained its full speed. My first and only ride in a steam locomotive became, for me, a real adventure. From my vantage point in the cab it appeared that the front of the very long engine was bucking and heaving and jerking from side to side. I couldn't believe that it was not about to jump the rails and go shooting off into the prairie. We must have been doing about sixty miles an hour. I was hanging on for dear life with the fireman and the engineer laughing their heads off at the paratrooper looking (and being) scared out of his wits. I soon realised that those guys were quite unconcerned with the violent movements of their charging monster. I hope they got the same kicks from watching the reactions of every person they invited up to ride with them. I suddenly developed a lot of respect for "Casey Jones."

I was glad to descend onto the platform when we arrived at Moose Jaw. I had to transfer to another railway, the Canadian

Pacific, for the short ride to Regina. The final leg of my journey home was the slowest as it was on a minor branch line of the Canadian National which ran from Regina up to Swan River three times a week. It stopped at every little village in between. With most of the time of my leave spent on trains both ways I still managed to have a couple of happy days with my mother and father and brother Paul.

On my return to Fort Harrison we spent the next couple of months honing our combat skills. We had two experts in unarmed combat. One tough looking customer was Captain O'Niell who had been on the Shanghai police force in China. He spent a lot of his time trying to teach us how to disarm anyone coming at us with a knife. Another was a fellow by the name of Guy D'Artois, a little French Canadian Captain who specialized in a lightning fast kick to the groin. I believe we all considered his as one technique worthy of mastering. If I were a gorilla like O'Niell I may have been more interested in his anti-knife technique.

We spent a lot of time on the range firing various weapons. One weapon we were taught to use was particularly repulsive. After we became fairly proficient in the use of the flame thrower I saw a news reel where one was used against a Japanese pill box fortification in the South Pacific. The footage showed the Marines shooting a stream of flames at a pill box and the occupants staggering out in flames and falling down. Fortunately we didn't carry any flame throwers in action.

The only other thing I never wanted to use was the respirator (gas mask). I mention the gas mask because I cannot remember a time during the five and a half years I was in the army that I was very far from that horrible appendage. We had to carry it at all times while dressed in "battle order." It was also mandatory while on leave in Britain. To be caught without it was an automatic charge and cancellation of leave.

CHAPTER 9

East: Virginia and Vermont

I n early April, 1943, the Force was being prepared for a completely new type of training and before long all leave was cancelled. While we were confined to camp there was a great flurry of packing and preparing to move out. On our second last day in Montana the Force had a great parade through the business section of downtown Helena.

It was our way of saying "Goodbye" to that most hospitable western city. After the parade there were many tearful farewells. It was evident that a fair number of our people were leaving wives and sweethearts behind.

The next day we entrained for a trip to Norfolk, Virginia. I understand it took five passenger trains and one freight train to transport our whole Force to the east coast.We were about to take the same "ship-to-shore" training as the U.S. Marines. Our new base was Camp Bradford near the entrance to Chesapeake Bay, about four miles out of Norfolk. The entire Norfolk area was alive with units of the American Navy, Army and Marine Corps. Ship-to-shore training was in preparation for the many sea borne invasions of enemy held territory which would be necessary if the Allies hoped to win the war.

We had left a part of the country where rattlesnakes were sometimes a problem. The swamps in the coastal areas of Virginia were apparently teeming with water moccasins, cotton mouths and the odd copper head. At least that was the impression our instructors were trying to leave with us. I could see that wading ashore in such an environment was going to be fun. Our training at Camp Bradford was under the direction of the U. S. Marine Corps. All of the reports we had heard about their "boot camps" certainly did not apply to that base. I suppose they respected the fact that we had no doubt had a "boot camp" or two in our own backgrounds. The training was, from my own point of view, enjoyable. We were all issued life belts which could be inflated by squeezing a trigger which punctured two carbon dioxide cylinders. Some of us had occasion to use them.

Most of our days in the beginning were spent loading into all steel landing craft and being ferried out to an old derelict three-masted sailing ship. It was anchored about a mile out in the bay. It was fitted out with "scramble nets" which hung from the deck down to water level about ten feet below. As the ship was anchored at a spot near the mouth of the bay there was often a substantial swell from the open ocean to our east. The height of the waves determined when it was considered safe for the training exercises to be carried out. On many occasions the sea was so rough that we would be soaked to the skin from the spray coming over the front of the landing craft as it plowed into the oncoming waves. The large swells also made coming alongside the old three master and climbing up the scramble net wearing full battle equipment a very dicey undertaking. Off loading into the assault boats for the rough trip to shore was even more challenging as we were being timed and judged on that performance. To the amazement of the Marine Corps our people were found to surpass their own beloved corpsmen in the alacrity with which we carried out that manoeuvre.

Our second week in the Chesapeake Bay area was spent aboard a troop transport which sailed up the bay and provided real life situations to further challenge our expertise in ship-to-shore work. The ship was named after a William P. Biddle. Most exercises from the Biddle were carried out during the darkness of night.

Shortly after the completion of our training at Camp Bradford we entrained for a new destination. To our surprise we headed north and finally arrived at Essex Junction, a small village just east of Burlington, Vermont. We marched the short distance from there to our new quarters, the barracks of Fort Ethan Allen. It was a typical well established army post. Everything about it was well kept. The buildings sparkled with new paint and the lawns were immaculate. It was close enough to Burlington to provide some rest and relaxation in the off hours.

At Fort Ethan Allen I shared a room at the end of our barrack block with a good friend by the name of Gerard H. Lee. He was a striking looking fellow being over six feet tall and with the trim body of an athlete. Because of a strip of white wavy hair which snaked back from his forehead he was known as "Silver" Lee. He was also very handy with his fists and had been First Division boxing champion while serving in England at the beginning of the war. "Silver" was the first sergeant of our fourth company, a rank equivalent to company sergeant major in the Canadian army. He outranked me in pay but for some reason I outranked him by being battalion operations sergeant. In the American army that was known as the battalion sergeant major even though my actual rank was staff sergeant.

"Silver" was one of the more colourful characters in the Force. I doubt there was a member among the twenty five hundred or so who did not know him by name. I like to feel that I was a guiding influence in his off-duty behaviour. It seemed that whenever he went to town with someone else he ended up tangling with the military police in some way or other. His value to the unit saved him from several scrapes with the law. I suggested to him that he shouldn't venture off the base without me and strangely he thought that was good advice—most of the time. "Silver" went on to win the American Silver Star for bravery during the South of France Campaign. He was first and foremost a soldier's soldier. I only saw

"Silver" several times since the war's end. He and his lovely wife Mickey were at our first reunion in Helena in 1947. He later joined the peacetime army and became a captain in the Governor General's Guard Regiment in Ottawa. He died in 1994.

Our training at Ft. Ethan Allen was more or less to put the finishing touches on our various skills. It included some strenuous night marches through the countryside hoping we could navigate by what maps we had, our compasses, and the stars. We also took part in some commando tactics such as crawling under barbed wire with live machine gun fire only a foot or two over our heads. We did lose one man, killed possibly by a faulty round which fell short. Accidents like that were all too common in the training I had in England. At that point the Force took in some new people who had not been through the training in the mountains nor the ship-to-shore exercises in Virginia. We were also joined at Ft. Ethan Allen by a artillery officer from Texas by the name of Edwin A. Walker. He was later to become Force Commander.

As Burlington was situated on a railway that ran north to Montreal and south to New York City it was customary for some to ask for passes to both cities whenever a weekend was allowed. They took the first train to come through the station whether it was going south or north. We did not have long to enjoy such privileges. We were soon declared ready for overseas service and packed our bags once again for a move which we thought would be to either North Africa or Britain. What a great surprise we received when the train we had boarded in Essex Junction, after going south towards New York for a couple of hours, switched to a track which was definitely heading west.

CHAPTER 10

West: San Francisco

Our trip to the west coast was the most Spartan of any of my train journeys in the U.S.A. We were in ancient passenger cars which had wicker benches to sit on. After trying to sleep on said bench for a couple of nights while sharing it with one other person it felt more like it was made completely of iron. By the time our train arrived in Denver, Colorado we were given a break. It consisted of a run through the streets for half an hour and deeply breathing that glorious mountain air. Refreshed we boarded the train for the last two days of our journey.

At the end of the fourth day we pulled into a dark and dreary side track which led into a huge pier on the San Francisco waterfront. After the usual interminable waiting period we were provided with a ferry boat on which we sailed out into the blackness of the bay. We slid past "The Rock", as Alcatraz was known to its underworld citizens. We had a first rate view of its menacing, well lit profile, thick walls, guard towers and barbed wire. Any Americans among us who were really considering a life of crime would have some second thoughts.

Little did we realize it but we were soon to land on the army's version of Alcatraz. Our ferry boat slid into the pier of another isolated land mass known as Angel Island. I believe the army post there was known as Fort McDowell. After debarking from the ferry we were marched up a very steep street, carrying everything we owned. At the top of the street we were herded into a large theatre and crowded into its seats which, with all of our gear, had standing room only. The next command was, "Take off all of your clothes." That was my first experience with being subjected to one of the U.S. army's long standing procedures, that of a compulsory "short arm" inspection for any troops entering a new post. They wanted to be sure none of us had any social diseases.

After the very tedious four days on the train, and periods of enduring humiliating procedures and documentations, we were finally assigned barrack blocks in which to have much-needed showers and a cot to sleep on. The one redeeming factor in our two weeks' stay on Angel Island was the food. The American army must have had a thing about "the condemned man ate a hearty meal." They certainly tried to live up to that credo as it turned out that most troops headed for the war in the Pacific were first billeted for a while on Angel Island. The food there was first rate. There was one other plus in being "incarcerated" on that island. Our laundry was done by the prisoners on "The Rock." I wondered if "Scar Face" Capone had ironed my shirts. I used the term "incarcerated" as there was absolutely no communication allowed between any of us and the outside world from that location. Some of our members could even see their homes across the water with their binoculars. They couldn't even make a phone call.

The two weeks there were not wasted as we spent a lot of time in speed marching on a very scenic road which circled the island at a good height. Besides toughening up the muscles a lot of distance can be covered by a body of troops using that system. We also spent a lot of time in caring for our weapons and brushing up on unarmed combat techniques. There are few places I can think of where the scenery was more spectacular than it was from the many view-points on that island.

Prior to our departure from Vermont we were issued clothing which would indicate that we would most likely be heading for one of the southern destinations—either Africa or the South Pacific.

That may have been an effort to confuse any possible security leaks in the East. As we prepared to leave Angel Island we turned in the warm weather clothing in exchange for something more indicative of a far Northern theatre of operations.

CHAPTER 11

Pacific Adventure—
The Aleutians

This chapter in my adventures in World War II actually began shortly after we boarded a brand new Liberty ship in San Francisco harbour. It was the middle of July in 1943. We had read a bit about Liberty ships. They were built in Oakland, just across the bay from San Francisco, in California. They were built in a hurry by an American industrialist by the name of Henry J. Kaiser. They were all welded construction rather than the usual method of riveting the steel plates together as most ships had been prior to that time. Rumour had it that some of them broke in two in a particularly heavy sea. That one was named the Nathaniel J. Wyeth in honour of a famous American painter of sea scapes.

We determined that the Wyeth was brand new. The possibility was that because of the wartime haste in such matters, it may not have been to sea for a trial run. Most ships built in peacetime are taken on a "shake-down" cruise to eliminate any "bugs" which may have been unnoticed during construction. It was questionable whether or not the Wyeth had experienced this treatment. Not only was the ship new but from what we were able to observe of the deck crew they appeared to be new to life at sea as well. We hoped that those who were located in vital spots such as the bridge and the engine room had earned their right to be there.

The excitement we experienced as we prepared to depart on that particular voyage was tempered by the knowledge that our training days were over. From then on we would undoubtedly be "playing for keeps." There was only one kind of destination we were then sure of and that would most certainly be somewhere near a Japanese-held island in the Pacific Theatre of Operations. Again, for security reasons we had not yet been informed of any specific destination. There were many to choose from in July of 1943.

When about one thousand men are stowed aboard a cargo ship of not much more than ten thousand tons there is not a lot of room left for recreational facilities. We and our gear were stashed below in compartments which had been designed for bulk cargo. Not the comfort you might expect on a regular cruise ship. Those compartments had been adapted, with the installation of folding steel and canvas bunks, to hold about two hundred men in each of five compartments or "holds." Washrooms and dining facilities were equally functional and austere. On board ship a washroom/toilet is referred to as the "head." Our particular "head" was located immediately above us on the main, all steel, deck. That particular area had not yet acquired the pungent odour of a real "head" as the ship was brand new.

With the newness of the "head" and its fairly large floor area, and the unlikelihood of an officer wandering in, it seemed like an excellent place for that great cure for boredom in the American forces—a crap game!—also known as "galloping dominoes." The game I am about to describe began like any other. A group of half a dozen or so had spread a ground-sheet on the deck and produced a pair of dice to begin the action. For a while it was just another crap game. Players came and had their turns. Some won and some lost and made way for new players. After a while it seemed that one particular roller, a Mexican-American named Gonzales, began to have all the luck. The pile of bills in front of him began to grow.

Normally when a fellow has made a "bundle" he draws some of his winnings as insurance that he won't lose his shirt. That guy was not touching any of his winnings but was letting it all ride.

He was shooting for the whole pot every time he picked up the dice. If anyone wished to cover what he had so far amassed they could place their bets hoping he would lose on his next roll. I hadn't really been counting but I would guess that by then he had successfully made about six or seven "passes." The odds were then very much against his making the next one. The time was ripe to cover whatever he was betting on the next roll. The size of the pot and the odds he would lose were a great incentive to "bet the farm"!

Most of the original players in the game had long since lost all of their cash and some of them stayed on only as kibitzers to watch the fun. Some were hurrying back to their respective quarters to find money to cover the crazy guy's bets. After a substantial amount of his pot was covered he rolled again. An eleven! He won again. The odds against him winning on his next roll were increasing with each roll of the dice. Anyone with money to bet would never have more favorable odds. By that time word of the crap game had spread like wildfire throughout the ship. New people were coming to reap their rewards. Others were scurrying around to find money to recoup their losses. To make a long story short, Gonzales made thirteen straight passes before the action ceased, no doubt for the lack of new takers. He may have cleaned out the ship!

One of his friends had the foresight to produce an empty kit bag for him to stuff his winnings into. It made a substantial bundle — something that would tempt any would-be thief. A rough estimation was that it may have contained as much as fifteen or twenty thousand dollars, a veritable fortune in 1943.

As he knew he couldn't stay awake to guard his treasure for the duration of a long ocean voyage he thought of an excellent solution to his problem. He took the kit bag full of money down into the engine room of the ship and paid one of the mechanics to weld the contents into a five-gallon jerry can. He then had him weld a short length of chain to the can. This he locked around his leg at night while he slept. It wasn't all that easy to keep track of during the days but he managed to disembark at our destination still possessing his treasure. The first night ashore he sneaked out of his tent while his buddies slept and buried the can in a spot known only to himself. Many questions would have been asked had he attempted to send that sum of money home through an Army Post Office; gambling in the service was strictly forbidden.

Shortly after the close of the game our ship pulled out of its pier. It was late in the afternoon as we passed under the spectacular Golden Gate Bridge and joined a convoy of several other troop ships and four destroyers. That was the 11th of July, 1943. I had been in the army since the 6th of June, 1940 and had not yet met the enemy other than being on the outskirts of a few air raids in Britain. Chances were that things were about to change, and not likely for the better.

As our convoy headed out into the open sea it soon became apparent that our ship was not a passenger liner. It rose and fell and rolled like a huge cork. Its cargo of men were no match as ballast for the heavy cargo it was designed to carry. The first night out it was my duty to stay awake near the only exit stairway to our hold as a security guard in case of fire or any other eventuality. The only light in the hold was over my position by the stairway. By that time I had adjusted my whole being to the somewhat violent pitching and rolling of the ship. Anyone unable to do so was by that time suffering from seasickness. I am told that if you are seasick long enough your most fervent wish is that the whole ship goes to the bottom as soon as possible. In all of my wartime journeys by ship I was able to avoid becoming seasick.

About midnight on my "watch" I was startled out of my wits by a terrible sound above our heads. There was a great rending, scraping noise followed by a louder crash. At the same time the light in our compartment went out. Visions of our ship breaking in half in this heavy sea flashed through my terror-stricken mind. The ship continued to roll and pitch and the rending and scraping noise soon had a pattern which indicated that a number of very heavy objects were rushing back and forth across the deck and crashing into the gunwales at each side of the ship.

That night seemed to last forever as by then the entire company in our area was awake and wondering what on earth was going on above. The almost ear-splitting din on the steel deck above our heads made sleep impossible. The uncertainty of what exactly was happening in the darkness above was enough to shake the faith of the most imaginative among us as to whether we would reach our destination or end our lives in a watery grave. There was little we could do in the darkness.

At first light the crew made their move to correct the situation as best they could. It appeared that there were about twenty 45 gallon drums of aviation oil stored on the deck for delivery to our island destination. They had not been secured as well as they should have been and the motion of the ship had loosened the cables which had secured them to one of the masts, eventually breaking the cable. By morning some of them were broken open and oil was all over the deck making it treacherous to walk anywhere in that area. Also the sea was still high and the oil drums were still rushing back and forth with enough power to kill anyone in their paths. It also became apparent that the initial slide of the drums had cut the power cable which provided light to our compartment.

The crew had produced high pressure water hoses and at great peril to themselves were managing to subdue the motion of one barrel at a time and get it overboard. This dangerous exercise took the better part of the morning. Fortunately no one was killed. The deck machinery was a wreck from the pounding it took all night. And finally the hosing down eventually made the deck relatively safe to walk on.

One morning, about two and a half weeks into our voyage, we were wakened by a sudden change in the throbbing rhythm of our ship's propellers. In fact the ship was vibrating as if the brakes were being applied. Some of us rushed up onto the deck to see what occasioned that action. It was a beautiful calm morning and directly in front of our ship was a beautiful little green island—scarcely fifty yards ahead. As we had been cruising for the past number of days over miles and miles of trackless ocean and no doubt navigating by compass and sextant there was probably no need for a lookout most of the time. It is also possible that we were in a part of this world which was not completely charted on existing maps. That may have been an island which had been missed by the cartographers of the time. It is also possible that the island could have been shrouded in fog as we approached it. The unexpected appearances of fog were phenomena to be reckoned with in the Aleutian Islands as we were soon to learn.

In any event it appeared that we were close enough to the island when it was spotted that there was insufficient room to turn the ship to avoid it. Hence the reverse action of our propellers. The ship came to a stop just short of running aground. Another few yards and it may have encountered some rather rocky bottom. Fortunately most of the islands in that part of the world were just the tops of mountains which had their bases many hundreds of feet below on the sea bed. We had just then encountered our first Aleutian Island, part of the chain which stretches from Alaska to just north of Japan.

Another phenomenon worthy of note in that part of the world was the extremely high amount of fluorescence in the sea water. This is caused by an overabundance of the tiny life forms which glow brightly when the water is agitated in any way. At night as we stood on deck and watched the other ships in our convoy we could see the hulls glowing as if lit by neon lights under each ship as it made its way. It was really something to see. We wondered at the time if any Japanese submarines would be attracted by those displays! Apparently not.

Towards evening of the same day we again saw land in quite another form. We had apparently at some time passed through the Aleutian Chain and had been sailing in the Bering Sea all day rather than the Pacific Ocean. The land we were then approaching was to our left. It consisted of a very high mountain which rose right out of the sea. It was an awesome sight. We had all seen mountains in Montana but their actual height is far more impressive when seen from sea level. While we were all feasting our eyes on that spectacle the wind moved a cloud bank and there behind the mountain we were gaping at was another peak almost twice as high! Very few sights are as impressive as the setting sun illuminating such a scene. We were then approaching the harbour of Adak.

Adak was one of the larger Aleutian Islands. At the time it was the major American base for operations against the Imperial Japanese Forces which had invaded the Attu and Kiska islands. It was very exciting to sail into the harbour and to observe the amount of military might that was assembled there. There were many ships at anchor in the harbour. There were warships of all sizes as well as a number of troop ships far larger than our Liberty Ship. There was also a constant flow of air traffic which consisted of bombers and fighters and sea patrol planes coming and going. We were at last in an operational theatre of war. We anchored in Adak harbour overnight and proceeded the next day on the final leg of our journey.

By mid afternoon we pulled alongside a dock on the island of Amchitka. Prior to our arrival at Amchitka we were informed that our mission was to be the spearheading of an attack on the Japanese held island of Kiska. Kiska was the last of the Aleutian Islands to be then occupied by the Japanese. Amchitka was to be our base for the operation as Kiska was only about 40 miles west of the western end of Amchitka.

When we had disembarked we proceeded to march, carrying everything we owned including our heavy kit bags. The loads we were required to carry at times led one of our members to refer to us as "Freddie's Freighters." Our overall commanding officer was a Colonel (later a Brigadier General) Robert T. Frederick. The name we called ourselves stuck for the remainder of the war. The names "Black Devils" and "Devil's Brigade" were tacked onto us later by the German army in Italy and some sensational writer or writers in the American news media—in that order. I personally never cared for either label.

We discovered after the first mile or two that our legs had softened considerably from the two weeks at sea. It seemed as if the tent covered area we were allotted was at least five miles from the harbour. The road we hiked on was merely earth from which the engineers had bull-dozed the gooey tundra to expose an almost as gooey dark brown mud.

We were soon to find that life prior to this had been a bowl of cherries, at least for those men who hadn't experienced a year, including a winter, in England with the Canadian infantry! Even so, morale was high and we were capable of taking a little suffering in our stride. Our sleeping quarters on Amchitka were U.S. Army tents. They were sixteen feet square and could each accommodate eight men on cots.

We were all issued mukluks, a waterproof boot that came half way up our calf. It was the only protection from the ever present mud, moisture and the foot-sucking tundra into which we sank over ankle deep with each step. At first it was a half-day's work, or so it seemed, just to go several hundred yards to the nearest mess tent for some food. The more enterprising of our members discovered that we could cut chunks of tundra and stack it by our stove to dry. It became fuel (apparently the same thing as good old Irish peat).

Most of our time was spent in studying the maps and sand table "mock-ups" of the island of Kiska. In this way we all learned to visualize the route we would take to reach our first objective after landing there in the dark of night. We also spent some time and ammunition in honing our skills with rifle and pistol and Thompson sub-machine gun.

About once a day we were treated to some great aerial displays as the fighter planes which were based to our east on Amchitka returned from their sorties over Kiska. They would come over our tents at "rooftop" level and waggle their wings as they roared past. I am certain that the jets of today's air forces wouldn't provide the same thrill for spectators that we experienced watching those P51 Mustangs and Kitty Hawks. One of the pilots who flew a Kitty Hawk fighter there is a friend of mine, Del English of Calgary. He later went to England and flew Typhoons to shoot up trains in Europe.

A week prior to our invasion of Kiska we were involved in a night exercise. Some time after midnight our battalion was loaded onto a destroyer that had been converted for the express purpose of assisting in rubber boat landings by a force such as ours. It was the U.S.S. Kane. For anyone who has read Herman Wouk's *Caine Mutiny*, the description of our Kane matches perfectly that of the Caine in the novel. There is no doubt in my mind that he used our ship as his model.

There were about two hundred men from our battalion on board the Kane as we sailed out of Amchitka harbour into the darkness. We were stowed below in very tight holds composed of folding bunks similar to those we experienced on the Wyeth out of San Francisco, only this time we were fully armed as if for combat, complete with packs and ammo and rifles and any other weapons needed. The only light in our hold was a dim red bulb. This was to condition our eyes for working on the deck in darkness as we launched our rubber boats.

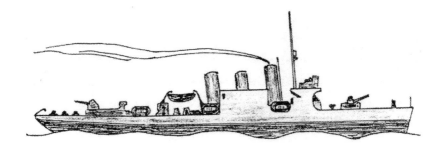

The U.S.S. Kane (drawing by Peter Cottingham)

We left Amchitka harbour a little after midnight and sailed northwest in the Bering Sea to a point about twenty miles up the island and about a mile and a half off shore. When the ship came to a stop we went up onto the deck. This was a rehearsal for the actual operation we were to take part in. We prepared to paddle ashore onto a beach on the north side of Amchitka. After lowering our rubber boats into the water, which was about six or seven feet below the deck of the destroyer, we climbed down the "scramble" nets and took up our pre-planned positions. We fanned out in a "vee" formation and began paddling towards the shore.

One of the reasons we had to paddle so far to reach the shore was because of the kelp. Kelp is a seaweed which grows in abundance off the shores of these islands. It has a stalk from the sea bed to the surface of the water which is as thick as a man's wrist. When it reaches the surface it becomes a long, flat leaf which floats in a mat which extends out from the shore, in some cases as far as a mile or so. Propeller driven boats have a hard time plowing through the stuff; hence the destroyer had to deposit us a considerable distance from shore.

After paddling for about an hour in the darkness we landed on a fairly smooth beach. As this was a practice run for the actual operation we spent some time discussing how we could have done it better and also in arriving at some consensus as to how much time we should allow ourselves for the landing. It was then about 4 o'clock in the morning.

We eventually broke open our rations and had an early breakfast. We waited for the first light of dawn at which time we were to paddle out to the Kane. As the sky began to lighten the Kane began to send us a message by Aldus Lamp flashes. That was the only time in the whole war that I was able to put my signal course (from Kingston) to any worthwhile use. The message I was able to read was as follows, "Enemy sub reported in area—must engage." The Kane then lay down a smoke screen and departed. We had no way of contacting them further and only hoped that they may have radioed base to tell someone to come out and pick us up. We could have gone back to base overland but we would have had to abandon the rubber boats. We needed them in our business.

We waited for two or three hours, but saw no sign of the Kane. Colonel Akehurst then decided that we should paddle out past the kelp and take a course parallel to the shore and head eastward towards the harbour. We estimated it to be about twenty or more miles distant. So we loaded our gear into the boats and paddled out past the kelp.

About this time one of the Bering Sea's famous fogs was descending on our group of paddlers. The weather in the Aleutians was probably the most unpredictable of any in the world. This was due to the two very different ocean currents which the Aleutian Chain bisected, the warm Japanese current of the Pacific and the frigid waters of the Bering Sea. Besides the fogs which we experienced many times in the several months there, we had what was called the "Williwaws." They were very strong winds which came out of nowhere with no warning from time to time. Those winds were responsible for many aircraft piling up, the pilots thinking they were landing into the wind, when suddenly the reverse would be the case.

As we were to follow in single file our boat remained at the rear of the column as we had the second in command of our battalion, Major Sulo V. Ojala, with us. He was one of the few with a compass so he chose to direct any stragglers. The fog became so thick that we could only see about forty yards. It was difficult to keep direction but we managed to keep in contact with the boats ahead of us and hope that someone ahead had a compass as well. After we had paddled for several hours things were getting a bit dicey. On one occasion we heard the engine of a fast boat approaching from our left (north) and we did not know if it was one of our motor torpedo boats or an enemy patrol. As we were all armed we decided that we would not fire on it until we could determine whose it was. As it passed just within our field of vision its ghostly outline in the fog looked completely alien. We determined that it may indeed have been an enemy patrol. We remained unseen to them.

We were later to learn from our navy that they had no craft of their own in that area at the time. It was even possible that they may have intercepted a message from our destroyer telling base to send someone out to look for us. Our rubber boats would have been juicy targets for the enemy had we been discovered.

As we paddled on we became thirsty and hungry and those of us who smoked were even out of cigarettes. We had been out for a lot more hours than we had banked on when we left the Kane so early in the morning. We had used all our of water in making coffee on the beach and by now had probably used most of the smokes in the group. We began to wonder if the Kane had radioed our predicament to base. Or if, in the presence of an enemy sub, they chose radio silence. Probably the latter.

About that time it was my turn to take a break from paddling. I was sitting in the back of the boat using my paddle as a rudder to keep the boat in the right direction. I heard a roaring sound from our rear. At first, I thought it was one of the large swells we were paddling in, breaking over a rocky outcropping near the shore. As I kept looking around I saw three huge walruses—heads, shoulders and tusks—come out of the sea about thirty yards away. They all raised their noses up and opening their mouths gave off a deep, fearsome roar. Quite a sound! I turned back to my companions and told them what I had seen.

While I was yelling at my companions to look, the group disappeared only to surface again in a matter of seconds, about twenty yards closer, repeating their intimidating roar in unison. This time we were all looking at them and contemplating what those shiny ivory tusks could do to our vulnerable inflated rubber boat. It was common knowledge by this time that any pilot who had to bail out into the Bering Sea had only minutes to inflate his seat pack dingy and climb into it. The Bering Sea was so cold that anyone immersed in it for more than ten minutes would die of hypothermia. We had no desire to give up our rubber boat at that point.

We held a hasty discussion with Major Ojala who had some knowledge of the wild animals of Alaska. He had spent some time with the Alaska Scouts in his earlier years. He seemed to know what he was talking about. It was generally agreed that we would be foolish to shoot them if they appeared again as they could do a lot of damage before our 30 calibre bullets took effect.

As we spoke they rose out of the water so close I could smell their breath. At such close range they were a terrifying sight. Their huge, wet, dark bodies were power personified and the nearness of their tusks to our fragile craft was most disturbing. The roar they gave out really put the cap on it. We were impressed to say the least! They were huge! They were awesome! I must admit that it was an incident which has been strongly imprinted in my memory.

One fellow in our boat, a radio operator accompanying a naval officer, had to be physically restrained from jumping overboard. He

"As we spoke they rose out of the water so close I could smell their breath.
At such close range they were a terrifying sight."

77

began to jabber in his strange Kentucky accent. He had really flipped, but it was hilarious to listen to him until we got him calmed down. He and his officer were detailed to land with our party during the actual invasion in order to call their ship for shell fire if we needed it. When the walruses disappeared the final time we could only wonder if they were conferring among themselves as to the best way to deal with the strange creature with a black bottom and six heads who had invaded their territory. If nothing else they were masters of suspense. We never saw them again but were sure left to wonder where they had gone and would they be back?

Shortly after the episode with the walruses the fog lifted and we found ourselves in a cove where the water was relatively calm. About a half mile away there was an Army tug which had been there some time using a derrick to retrieve a downed aircraft from the sea. Our Colonel, Jack Akehurst, was in a boat at the head of our column and was the first one to reach the tug.

He made arrangements for them to tow our rubber boats back to port. At that point we were pretty hungry and thirsty and tired from the miles we had paddled. We were being rescued at last.

It was decided that we would tie our boats, one behind the other in three or four different "strings" to the rear rail of the tug boat. By climbing over the boats ahead we could board the tug. Most of the men scrambled over the boats ahead of them until they were safely on the deck of the tug. From my point of view I saw nothing wrong with staying in my boat and riding back to the harbour in that manner. My boat was at the tail end of one string. It was probably the next thing to, if not the dumbest, move I ever made.

As the tug proceeded towards the harbour, which was still five or six miles away, the rubber boats strung out behind it followed nicely in their separate lines jostling each other from time to time.

It appeared that the tug that was pulling our boats was of sufficiently shallow draft that it could operate close to the shore and was not hindered by the fibrous stalks of the kelp. This was bad news for the boats being pulled along and for anyone crazy enough to be riding in one of them. The propellers of the tug were chopping up the stalks of kelp and leaving a very rough trail to follow. I noticed one of the rubber boats to my right starting to spin in its tracks like the lure on the end of a fishing line. One of its corner ropes had come off allowing it to meet the oncoming turbulence of the water and chopped kelp at an angular approach. Had anyone been sitting in that boat he would have been thrown out into some of the coldest water in the world.

On seeing what was happening to the other boat I tried to draw the attention of someone on the tug to my own predicament. But with the noise of the diesel engines no one heard my shouts. Besides I was about forty yards behind the tug. To my great consternation the rope at the left front shoulder of my boat came untied and my own boat assumed a somewhat diagonal approach to the oncoming fiber-filled waves. I spent the next terrifying hour or so in the center of the boat throwing my weight against any direction that the boat bucked in its attempt to start flipping over. Needless to say I was all in, physically and mentally, when we finally slowed on our way into the harbour.

About three or four days prior to our actual invasion of Kiska our training officer decided that we should really get into shape. He ordered our regiment to complete a very strenuous overland march in full battle equipment. This involved hiking about twenty miles west on the island and returning to camp without a rest. A total of about forty miles over tundra! As mentioned before, tundra is not your regular kind of walking. I have been on some real route marches in my day. In England with the Regina Rifle Regiment there were many days when we had to march here and there across Southern England on schemes (manoeuvres) sometimes twenty, thirty, and as many as forty miles in a 24 hour period. Sometimes in the rain or snow, mostly on hard surfaced roads which jarred the brains out of us as our boots all had steel clad heels.

Once in Montana we marched fifty-one miles in seventeen hours. Half of that distance was on a railway track where the ties aren't quite the right distance apart for a decent footstep. At least on that gruelling march we were wearing the beautifully engineered parachute boots.

I can't swear that we did the whole twenty miles up the island before we paused for refreshments and headed back to camp. But those of us who were reading the map were fairly sure of where we turned around. I recall that many times on that hike I was quite sure that I could not go another step. As dawn approached life became a painful blur of pulling one foot out of the muck and putting the other ahead of it.

The only incentive to keep going was the bare faced reality that there were no vehicles coming behind us which could pick up the stragglers. Every time we came to the top of a distant hill we expected to see our tents. All we saw was another series of hills extending to the horizon. I can truthfully say that I have never been so completely exhausted as I was on that exercise.

Eventually we managed to get to the crest of a hill where we could see our tents in the distance. By that time we were all operating on pure will power. Putting one foot in front of the other was taking every ounce of effort we could muster. I was the first one of our HQ detachment to reach our tent and I literally crawled into it on my hands and knees. My first action was to reach for several cans of "C" rations from a crate under one of the cots. I punched holes in their tops to keep them from exploding and placed them on top of our pot-bellied stove. I lit a fire in it and fell fast asleep on my cot.

As the rest of our group crawled in we finally managed to get the tops off the cans and take on some nourishment. Nothing ever tasted as good as that can of beans and hash. A couple of days to rest up and we were ready for the invasion of Kiska! I'm not sure, nor is anyone else who took part in that exercise, that we were in better shape than we may have been without it.

The remainder of our time on Amchitka was spent in further study of maps and sand-table displays of our objective. Particular attention was paid to making sure that all the weapons we would be carrying were properly cleaned, oiled, and ready for use. Reports from our air patrols still indicated that there was plenty of anti-aircraft fire thrown up in their direction whenever they got over Kiska. Strangely enough I don't recall that any of our men showed signs of trepidation about the mission we were about to take part in. It was part of knowing that we had some of the most intense training of any unit which would be involved. As mentioned before, the excitement was tempered by knowing that the invasion of Attu several months before had been a very costly operation in terms of American casualties.

First Regiment, of which our battalion was a part, was to participate in the sea borne landings. Our mission was to land by rubber boat at a certain cove on the north shore of Kiska under cover of darkness, scale the cliffs and make our way to the top of the mountainous ridge which ran the length of the island. We knew from aerial photos that there were enemy positions on or near the tops of all the high parts of the ridge. The main Japanese installations, including some very heavy artillery, were on the south side of the island. Those fortifications also included their airstrip, seaplane base, naval base, barracks and supply depots.

Our second regiment was to stand by at the air strip on Amchitka with their parachutes on ready to board the transports and drop onto the island about five miles to our left if we radioed that we needed this diversion. All the plans so far were well conceived to assure an overwhelming superiority in numbers once the operation got under way. From the look we had at the amount of naval and air support in the harbour at Adak we felt confident that we would have a better chance of survival than the force that went against Attu, an island west of Kiska that had recently been taken from the Japanese at a very high cost in American casualties.

13th of August, 1943. Final preparations were completed by late afternoon as we boarded the U.S.S. Kane for what we expected would prove to be our of "Baptism of Fire." We sailed out of Amchitka harbour under cover of darkness. According to the map I was studying we would have to cross the international date line, 180 degrees west of Greenwich.

CHAPTER 12

The Kiska Invasion

O ur ship, again the same U.S.S. Kane, rounded the island of Kiska from the southwest and at about twenty minutes past midnight on August the 14th, 1943, we were ready to launch our rubber boats.

This was the moment I had spent the last three years training for. It was high adventure the likes of which I had only read about. As we were only a little over half a mile from the enemy shore we tried to be as quiet as possible in launching our boats over the side of the Kane. This done we scrambled down the nets into them and fanned out into the planned formation for paddling to the shore.

Everything was going according to plan when the clouds, which had covered this part of the world for what seemed like weeks, finally parted and revealed a very large and bright moon. We had really been counting on darkness. As if this hadn't changed our confident outlook some idiot on one of the naval ships decided to fire a round from a very large calibre gun. That really started the old adrenaline flowing. We fully expected from that moment to be met with at least a hail of machine gun fire from the slowly approaching shore.

After some very tense moments of paddling a little faster we reached the rocky shore and began to scramble out of our boats. At that point I was again amazed at either the ignorance, or was it nonchalance of some of our people, who, upon reaching the shore let their weapons clatter as they threw them down between the rocks

Kiska Island

and casually had a leak. Does the bladder's reaction to nervous tension override the fear of being shot?

The "cliff" we had anticipated having some difficulty with was really not a bad climb. There were plenty of hand and foot holds and we didn't have to use the ropes as we had figured. Soon our entire landing party was on its way, as yet unopposed, towards our objective at the top of the mountainous ridge.

About half-way up the mountain one of our people had the misfortune to misfire the new Johnson machine gun. It was a weapon manufactured for the Marine Corps, but issued to a few of our people to try out on this operation. Hearing a burst of machine gun fire at that point most outfits, we were to learn, would have been pinned to the ground and possibly firing some of their own weapons at possible targets, believing they were under attack. I was proud of those guys. No one seemed overly concerned and in a businesslike manner determined that what had happened was a fluke in the safety mechanism of an experimental weapon. We continued our upward climb without further incident.

We finally reached a point where we could see the opening to the enemy bunker on the peak of the ridge. We spread out and keeping low approached it warily. We determined that as the round fired earlier from the destroyer and the burst of machine gun fire hadn't alerted anyone to be visibly defending this bunker, it must be empty. As we neared it we could see in the open door facing us that there appeared to be no one inside.

We had the strangest feeling as we entered that the bunker had been very recently occupied. This was confirmed as we felt the stove. It was warm and contained a pot of luke warm coffee on top. At that moment, which was 6 a.m., there was a terrific explosion from the direction of the shore where we had landed.

A section from our first battalion had been detailed to follow us and clear a way for heavier landing craft to come ashore. The cove they were to land in was guarded by several rock outcroppings. Our people had the job of planting enough Ryan Special explosive around those rocks to blow a path to the beach. From the sound of the explosion they may have opened a channel deep enough to run a destroyer up to the shore! As it happened they were quite successful and in no time apparently there was a succession of craft coming in with everything from bull dozers to a field hospital.

At precisely the same moment as the detonation to our north sounded, the American navy began to shell the main harbour installations on the south side of the island. At that time the ship-to-shore party which had accompanied our HQ to our present position set up their radio for communicating to the battle cruiser they were from. In attempting to reach their ship by radio all they could hear at that moment seemed to be an enemy transmitter using the same frequency. They could hear the American shells bursting and some very excited Japanese language, an indication that some of the enemy were still in the main camp. They were unable to reach the cruiser with their radio until later. At that time they communicated the fact we had found evidence of a recent evacuation of the bunker we were now in.

The American intelligence had their own agenda and to this day they insist that the enemy had left the island en masse a day or two before our arrival. I think the navy would have been embarrassed to admit that some had slipped through the "ring of steel" which we were to observe the first time the fog lifted. The island was surrounded by the largest concentration of various American warships, landing craft and troop carriers I had ever seen.

Towards the end of our first day on the island we were being relieved by the 87th Mountain Infantry unit from the USA. We made our way back down the mountain to a valley about half a mile inland from the point the supplies were being unloaded. At that time it was not conceded that the island was completely in friendly hands and that was most unfortunate because the troops of the 87th must have had the wits scared out of them prior to coming ashore behind us. Their first night on the island the fog closed in and made visibility very deceptive.

As a consequence there was a lot of small arms fire being exchanged between various companies of the 87th, some of whom were dug in on the rim of our small valley. I can remember crawling from pup tent to pup tent where our fellows were bivouacked and telling them that the only weapons we had heard sounded very much like "friendlies." I advised them to hold their fire until any movement was proven to be enemy.

The firing lasted most of the night and we began to wonder if there was more to it than some trigger-happiness in the ranks of the 87th. Dawn was to reveal that it was sadly one of the worst cases of "trigger happiness" that any outfit ever experienced. There was a steady procession of litter bearers coming past us carrying the dead and wounded from that "friendly" exchange. Apparently some sections had shot every group which came up to relieve them thinking they were the enemy. We counted at least thirteen dead being carried past. In a movie documentary of an 87th reunion in Denver that I watched a few years ago a much larger body count than thirteen was revealed. Not one of our people had been doing any of the firing, nor were any of them shot.

By mid morning of our second day on the island the navy Sea Bees (engineers) had built a road inland as far as our bivouac. It was amazing to see what had been off loaded onto the shore in the way of supplies in such short order—a very impressive display of American wealth and know-how in action.

After spending about five days in our very wet, and for August, very cold bivouac area, living two men to a pup tent, we were finally ordered to trek across the central ridge of mountains and down the south side to the main camp area. By now the high command was reasonably sure there were no enemy troops on the island. Our stand-by 2nd regiment were not required to make their parachute jump in our support. I think they were slightly disappointed to have missed out on the whole operation. They remained back on Amchitka as far as I know, later to join us in Adak for the trip back to San Francisco.

We moved out in small groups taking different routes to get over the high ground with orders to keep a lookout for any signs of enemy stragglers. In this way we could be reasonably sure that a lot of country would come under surveillance. We arrived at a beach about a half-mile west of the main installations at about three o'clock in the afternoon. That was to be our assembly area for transfer to an ocean liner which was to be our transportation back to the States.

We had plenty of time to kill waiting for our next move. That gave us a chance to look over some of the Japanese installations which were then in a shambles from the air bombing and the naval bombardments. There were several miniature submarines still in their ways and ready for launching except for the holes which the departing enemy had blown in their hulls. The large calibre coastal guns in emplacements here and there were also destroyed. They were British-made and may have been captured in Hong Kong or Singapore.

While waiting on the beach I observed a most bizarre action by a supposedly trained soldier. I could hardly believe my eyes as some idiot proceeded to dig out an anti-tank mine from the sand of the beach. It had been partially exposed by the action of the tide and the waves. Having dug it out he then proceeded to hammer the detonator button on its top with his entrenching tool (a small folding shovel). Had it not been corroded by the salt water I would not likely be writing this now as he was only seven or eight yards from me at the time.

I hollered at him to stop while those of us in the vicinity scampered away from the nut. When I look back on it I should have had him placed under arrest as I was probably the senior NCO in the area at the time. Had it detonated there would have been a fairly large crater in the beach where he had been and who knows how many casualties near it. So much for the hand of fate. It was doubtful that a character like he would survive the mines and booby traps the German Army had planned for him in the Italian campaign.

Shortly after that harrowing episode we were loaded into a tank landing craft and made our way through the now dark and rainy evening out to a waiting liner that was anchored about a mile off shore in a very heavy sea. As we drew alongside of the liner it became evident that boarding her would be a very dicey exercise as the heavy swells were raising and lowering our metal craft many feet as it ground against the steel sides of the big ship.

To make matters worse for me I was carrying not only my own heavy gear but an extra rifle as well. One of my friends, Tommy Cole, had to go off with Colonel Akehurst on some errand and I offered to watch his rifle for him. He hadn't returned by the time it was our turn to leave the beach so I had two rifles to carry as I climbed the scramble net to reach the deck of the liner, a climb equal to about four stories up a building. A scramble net was a very wide rope ladder, several of which hung from the sides of troop ships involved in ship-to-shore landings. In this case it was tricky to grab the net at the top of a swell which lifted the landing craft and climb fast enough to avoid having the craft come up higher on the next swell and cut a leg off. One of our number was not quite fast enough and almost lost a leg as it was jammed between the two vessels. He fell screaming, back into the smaller craft, and had to be loaded with a winch and stretcher.

By midnight all of our people had been settled on board the J. Franklin Bell, as our liner was known. It was part of the President Lines fleet which sailed from west coast ports to Hawaii and the Orient during peacetime. It was another luxury liner which had been converted to wartime troop carrying.

The next morning we weighed anchor and set off in an easterly direction anticipating that our first port of call would of course be our base at Amchitka. Towards evening it became apparent that we had bypassed Amchitka as we were sailing once more into the harbour at Adak. We were to learn that our Service Battalion had picked up our barracks bags back at base and had shipped them to our next stateside destination.

As our friend of the "crap game", Gonzales, had buried his treasure on Amchitka hoping to be back there to retrieve it, he was now in a great state of anxiety. There was next to no chance of his ever being back in that part of the world again. However, the First Special Service Force being the kind of outfit it was, Hector's colonel got wind of his predicament and did a little inter-service scrounging on his behalf. It so happened that the U. S. Navy had a PBY flying boat which was about to deliver an important person to Amchitka and return to Adak that day. As our ship was not due to leave port for another day arrangements were made to transfer Gonzales to the PBY for the flight to Amchitka. He was back on board the J. Franklin Bell by late afternoon with his five-gallon can of money.

A surprising sequel to the story of the crap game presented itself to me in a locale about half a world away from the Aleutian Islands. I found myself in a crap game in a rest area in Italy. One of the principals happened to be Gonzales. He had done very well in that game as he had on board the Nathaniel Wyeth, but the stakes did not compare with those of the former game. We were playing with the "Occupation Lira" of poor old Italy. There were only a half dozen of us involved. As the rest of the players drifted away, Hector and I were left to rehash the events of the evening.

I made some comment about his great string of luck aboard the troop ship. He kept rolling the dice on the blanket which was still on the floor in front of him. He finally looked up and said, "What would you like me to roll, Pete?" At first I didn't know how to take such a remark and then it dawned on me that he was serious. A light began to glow in my dim mind. I answered him saying, "How about an eight?" Without answering he just rolled and up came an eight. I began to watch his movements more closely. I noted that he showed a great deal of dexterity as he picked up the dice. He continued to impress me as he called his own shots for a while with an amazing degree of accuracy.

He then went on to explain that as a teenager he had been incarcerated in one of America's southern jails for a misdemeanor which would probably have earned him a mere fine had he not been of Mexican descent. As it was, he served several months as a guest of Uncle Sam. While so occupied he shared a cell with an old riverboat type who knew his way around a crap table and was happy to teach his young roommate. He spent many hours learning the skill of how to pick up the dice and roll them out with the best chance of having them tumble to a stop in his favour.

He explained that first of all, to avoid "crapping out" on the first roll by rolling either *snake eyes*, a deuce or three, or *box cars,* a twelve, you have to place the dice just so when you pick them up. Have the sixes face-to-face, or the aces face-to-face and do so quickly so as not to arouse suspicion. They're likely to roll out the same way if you're skillful enough, and thus avoid crapping out on the first roll. I had to admire his skill.

Was he a cheat? On thinking it over I had to admit that he was not. He had enough self-discipline to learn a real skill which proved to be quite useful in the real world, a world in which those of us without his skill merely trusted luck in an attempt to get something for nothing—other people's money.

CHAPTER 13

Slow Trains

The next day in the company of several other ships, including the U.S.S. Missouri, we set off in convoy for the United States. Our trip back was much faster than the one out in the Liberty Ship. The most noteworthy thing about that trip was the thrill of watching the Missouri, the largest battleship in the world, as she plowed through the heavy swells of the North Pacific. An awe inspiring sight I never tired of.

The last day of our voyage back to the States we lost the company of the Missouri as she was diverted to her home base of Bremerton, Washington. We still had an escort of a couple of destroyers which accompanied our convoy under the Golden Gate Bridge and into San Francisco's magnificent harbour. We docked at about 4 o'clock in the afternoon. Disembarking in San Francisco we had another of the army's long waits as those in charge of such matters finally arranged for us to load onto a ferry boat. By the time we got under way again it must have been at least midnight. Our ferry boat proceeded out into the darkness guided only by illuminated channel markers as we made our way up the Sacramento River. After what seemed like a couple of hours our boat swung out of the channel into a dimly lit wharf in a place named Pittsburgh. We disembarked.

We then proceeded to march, again quite hungry and thirsty and heavily laden with packs and gear. We made our way through the dimly lit streets of Pittsburgh for a couple of miles and into what appeared to be a football stadium. The stadium was designed for night games and the high bank of lights on the east side of the stands were all lit up illuminating center field like daytime. However, the dugout area next to the stands was in darkness and there was a line of cars parked there facing the field. We could see cigarettes glowing in the darkness behind their windshields.

As we lined up at center field a loud speaker instructed us to remove all of our clothing. Having heard the same command on previous occasions we all knew what to expect. We were going to experience another "short arm inspection;" the army's euphemism for a check for V.D. As we made our naked way past the inspecting staff seated at their various tables we could only guess the gender of the owners of the glowing cigarettes in the parked cars.

We eventually donned our clothes and were marched another mile or so to a place called Camp Stoneman, a receiving depot for troops returning from the Pacific. After a good night's sleep we were issued tickets for individual travel, in my case, via Canada to Burlington, Vermont. I marvelled at the efficiency of this operation as every man in our outfit was given a ticket to his home address. That involved a large staff of army office workers in conjunction with various railway agents, a truly great demonstration of logistical cooperation. We had people from all parts of the US and Canada to be looked after.

The first leg of my journey was to Vancouver, thence to Regina where I caught a train to Swan River, Manitoba,for a visit with my mother and father and brother Paul. Time was a very precious thing as we all had to be back in Fort Ethan Allen, Vermont, by a certain date. I believe that I only had a couple of days at home before it was time to leave.

That was the third time that I had to say "Good Bye" to my parents prior to proceeding overseas. Now being a parent myself I can only surmise how desperately hard it was for them during the war. Before it was to end they were to have had five of their sons in uniform with three of them overseas, one of whom was never to return. Fortunately the war ended before the two youngest, Frank in the Army, and Duncan also in the Army, could be shipped overseas.

Prior to our disembarking in San Francisco we were all put on notice that we were slated for overseas duty again. In the American Army that meant that anyone late returning to his post would be charged with desertion. They didn't fool around. As it happened most of us were able to get back to Vermont on time with the exception of a very good friend of mine, "Spud" Wright.

"Spud" was paraded up in front of his battalion commander being charged with desertion. His commander, Lt. Col. Beckett asked him if he had anything to say for himself and he replied, "Yes Sir, slow trains and fast women." His case was dismissed. "Spud" went on to become one of the most decorated and best loved men in our outfit. He was promoted to officer rank during our campaign in Italy.

It was September and we were back in our old post at Fort Ethan Allen for regrouping, and some more training. That time it was about what to expect from the Germans. We were also issued new equipment to replace any which had been lost or damaged in the Aleutians. That included a new jacket more suitable to climate and terrain of southern Europe. Shortly we were again ready to proceed overseas.

CHAPTER 14

Overseas Again

About the middle of October we travelled to Camp Patrick Henry, Virginia. Enroute to Virginia our train took us through a tunnel under the New York harbour and when we surfaced on the New Jersey side we had a glimpse of the rusty hulk of the once glamorous Normandie being towed to its final destination, a scrap yard where it would be cut up and recycled for the many tons of steel it contained.

A short week later we were trucked to Newport News, Virginia. where we embarked on a beautiful Canadian Pacific liner now bearing the name Empress of Scotland. That ship had sailed from Vancouver to the Orient in peacetime as the Empress of Japan but as we were now at war with Japan it seemed prudent to change the name. The name change did not alter the beautiful decor on board which was done in exotic woods and quite distinctly Japanese in every way.

On the 28th of October we set sail from one of America's largest naval bases to the strains of a Marine Corps band which was playing on the wharf as we slid out of our berth. A very emotional send-off. This time we were sure that a lot of us would not be coming back. We were headed for the Italian Campaign. The place which Winston Churchill had referred to as the "Soft underbelly of Europe." I expect that he lived to regret his use of that terminology.

As the Empress was another of the faster ships of her time we sailed unescorted across the ever dangerous Atlantic. I can't recall being overly concerned for our safety on that voyage. One complete deck on that ship was "off limits" to the men of the Force.It contained a large contingent of WAC's (American Women's Army Corps). I can't imagine why that whole deck was "off limits" to nice guys like us.

On the 5th of November we sailed into Casablanca, that fabled North African center of intrigue and espionage. The harbour at Casablanca was a scene of nautical desolation probably only surpassed by Pearl Harbour after the 7th of December, 1941. There were masts and funnels of countless ships protruding from the waters of its harbour everywhere one looked. Our ship finally berthed on the opposite side of a pier at which France's pride and joy, the Jean Bart lay inoperable. Rather than let it fall into German hands the ship had been scuttled by her crew. They had opened her sea-cocks and flooded the engine rooms allowing her to settle on the bottom. It was one of two identical battleships of which the French Navy boasted. In the shallow water of her berth she appeared to be only riding low in the water. We were soon to meet her sister ship under like conditions at the Mediterranean port of Oran in Algeria.

As I was disembarking from the ship I casually flipped the glowing butt of my cigarette onto the concrete floor of the dock. To my surprise about four lurking figures sprang out of the shadows and pounced upon it. The winner came up with the butt, took a deep drag on it, snuffed it out and with a satisfied smile tucked it into his drawers. Welcome to Africa, Peter. That incident was to appear quite tame and ordinary over the revelations of the next few days.

We were soon herded into what appeared to be an early model of a freight train. The box cars were known to the French Foreign Legion as the "Forty & Eights" as they were usually occupied by either forty men or eight horses. Standing room only. Fortunately for us we did not have to be so crowded. As I recall, for the three days and three nights that we were guests of that railroad, we were able to take turns stretching out to sleep while half of our number huddled in a sitting position in one end of the car.

Some of the highlights of that trip included brief stops at cities such as Rabat, Fez and Sidi-Bel-Abbes, famous names in the annals of the Foreign Legion. Another experience of note was in proceeding through the longest tunnel in the Atlas Mountains. The train was pulled, not all that swiftly, by a coal burning midget (by our standards) locomotive and what with the dense smoke and steam we seemed to be forever in that tunnel trying to breathe. We even tried donning our gas masks but that only added to our sense of claustrophobia. I was impressed, but not amused...

CHAPTER 15

On to Italy

At the end of our third day we arrived at the city of Oran on the Mediterranean coast of North Africa, We were then in fabled Algeria. That part of the world had only recently been taken from the occupying Germans by the American 5th Army under the command of General Mark Clark. He was to be our Army Commander in Italy. We were housed in tents several miles out in what appeared to be the edge of the Sahara Desert southeast of Oran. My only memory of that God-forsaken spot was that we found it prudent to shake our boots well before putting them on in the morning. Scorpions had a way of liking the cozy feeling of spending the night in a parachute jump boot.

On the 16th of November we were trucked down to the docks of Oran and loaded onto the Thomas Jefferson, (one of the smaller liners that part of our unit trained on in the Chesapeake Bay). By a strange coincidence that ship was berthed right next to the identical sister ship of the Jean Bart of Casablanca. It was the Richelieu and had also been scuttled in such a manner that it still appeared to be seaworthy at first glance.

Our convoy of half a dozen troop ships and several escorts sailed without incident to Naples, Italy, where we docked on the 19th of November, 1943. The highlights of that voyage were that each ship in our convoy was towing a large barrage balloon to protect it from radio controlled bombs which the Luftwaffe was often using against ships in the Mediterranean at the time. The balloons had a steel cable tethering them above and to the rear of the ships making it unattractive to get too low with a plane. The other highlight was in sailing past the Isle of Capri and Mount Vesuvius as we approached Naples harbour.

After disembarking in Naples and marching, fully loaded, about five miles to a bivouac area north of the city we pitched our pup tents in a valley which contained much of the detritus of battle. A lot of destroyed German Army motorized equipment and artillery hardware was evident everywhere. One could only guess at the kind of battle which had taken place there in the not too distant past. After spending the night there we were trucked to what was to become our base of operations for the mountain campaign on the Cassino Front.

Our new temporary home turned out to be the former barracks of an Italian Army Artillery School at a place named Santa Maria di Capua, about 40 miles north of Naples. The Germans had occupied it prior to being driven further north and in leaving had destroyed the ends of each block which contained the stairways to the second floors. The piles of rubble they left just gave us a little more practice at our favorite sport—mountain climbing.

By December the 2nd we were ready to proceed to the front line. Our first mission was to assault the massive Mount La Difensa and wrest it from the Germans who held the high ground there. It guarded the approaches to the city of Cassino which was in the entrance to the Liri Valley and beneath the mountain on which sat the famous Benedictine Monastery of Monte Cassino. That was considered the most impregnable strong point on the Gustav line. During the night of the 2nd we moved into position for the assault on Difensa under cover of darkness which was punctuated by one of the most concentrated artillery barrages of the entire Italian campaign. Difensa was later written up in Life magazine as the "Million Dollar Mountain." Relating to the cost of the barrage no doubt! The entire south facing top of the mountain was alive with shell bursts for hours and hours that night as our 2nd Regiment prepared to assault it from the steep cliffs under the top as soon as our own shellfire ceased.

As I was in 2nd battalion, 1st Regiment, it was our lot to be the back-up for 2nd Regiment's assault on the peak. We moved half way up the mountain under cover of darkness and rested there out of sight of the enemy forward observers waiting for word from the 2nd Regiment as to when we should proceed further in our support of their mission. It was late in the afternoon of the 3rd of December that we received orders to move out. There was apparently some confusion in the mind of the person or persons directing our order of march; as we rounded the northeast face of the mountain it was not yet quite dark. It was later proven that in so doing we were in direct view of the enemy's forward observers to our north.

In a very short time, after holding their fire, they had the entire 2nd battalion in their sights as we rounded the corner and were strung out in a line across their front. By that time it was becoming quite dark but they had fired a few rounds of white phosphorous into our midst which gave them ample time to adjust their range and really pour it on. In the darkness and rain that was falling all pandemonium let loose. We began to experience the heaviest concentration of artillery and mortar fire that any of us were to encounter for the rest of our war in either Italy or later in France.

Because of the total darkness and rain and the terrible clamour of incoming shells it was difficult to attend to the wounded. It is impossible to describe the terror which the sound of even one incoming artillery shell can instill in a person. Anything which is going to land within fifty yards of you sounds like it will land right on you. The entire area in which we found ourselves was a cauldron of exploding shells, flying rock fragments and men all over the place screaming for medics. The ground we occupied was so rocky that digging any kind of a shelter from the shrapnel was next to impossible.

That was a night which changed our outlook on this world forever. It is one thing to face what appeared to be certain death for a minute or two as so often happened during the rest of the war but it was another to face it in what seemed like an eternity as was the case that night. The shellfire was relentless for hours and hours. The miracle was that any of us survived to tell about it.

One thought kept running through my mind during all of that and it was related to the concentrated special talent of my superbly trained battalion being wasted as cannon fodder in such a seemingly useless exercise which could have had very little effect on the final outcome of our war with Germany. Our expertise was totally wasted in that type of operation. The enemy would have had a great propaganda coup had they realised what their artillery was destroying that night.

Eighteen men in my battalion were killed in that barrage and fifty odd were wounded including myself. A few of the others, who were neither killed nor wounded, were taken out as badly shell-shocked. Some of the latter were never seen again by any of us until the odd one made his appearance at recent reunions.

Because of the decimation our battalion received that night the remnants were unable to be of much help in supporting the efforts of 2nd Regiment. Fortunately 2nd Regiment was able to secure the high ground and clear it of the enemy at considerable expense in men killed and wounded.

As mentioned, I was among those wounded in the La Difensa fiasco. About half-way through the night a very close shell burst resulted in something striking the sole of my boot with a great force. It felt as if someone had hit the arch of my instep very hard with a hammer. I assumed it was a flying rock as there was a lot of rock and shrapnel flying around. I really didn't feel any pain at the time. I checked the fellow lying beside me in the mud to see if he was OK. He was.

Another near explosion plastered my face with a mixture of mud and apparently phosphorous from one of their "marker" shells. The mud glowed in the dark and it had been driven into my nose and ears by the concussion of the blast. Fortunately it didn't get into my eyes which were closed tightly at the time. I was later to experience the results of the phosphorous in a couple of ways which were not too pleasant.

Just before daybreak the shelling finally let up. The enemy must have run out of ammunition for their guns as when the day brightened we were quite visible to their forward observers and must have presented an even better target than in the black of night. There was a most welcome break in the action.

What a miserable looking lot we were. We still had to endure the cold drizzle. Litter bearers were making their way up the trail in groups of four and picking up the wounded here and there. It was a scene of complete desolation. I found myself envying the dead. They were out of the war. Those of us who could walk were getting up from the prone position and making our way back down the trail towards the east side of the mountain where we would not present such a juicy target for the guns to our northwest. As I made my way I began to feel sharp pains in my foot and it bothered me that I would have to carry on in such pain but so many of our number were obviously so badly wounded that I would feel ridiculous seeking aid for what I thought to be a nasty bruise.

As I approached Colonel Akehurst to find out what our next move was I was met by my friend and assistant battalion operations sergeant, Charlie Dawson. He looked at my left boot and drew my attention to the blood which was oozing out of the top of my instep. I hadn't bothered to look at it prior to that moment and was surprised to see the blood. I had assumed I had only been hit on the bottom of the foot by a rock. A team of litter bearers came along and the medic in charge suggested that I remove my boot so they could have a look at my foot. That was a mistake as I think I could have made it down the trail by myself if the boot was left on. When I removed the boot my foot swelled up and it appeared that a small piece of shrapnel had passed right through my instep. To have had sufficient force to penetrate the heavy composition of the sole of my boot and my ankle as well, so small a segment must have been propelled from very, very close. No wonder I felt so shell-shocked. I couldn't get the boot back on so they decided to put me on the stretcher and carry me down the mountain to the aid station at the bottom.

As they were carrying me down the trail the enemy must have received a new load of ammo because the shelling began again. A shell which appeared to be coming really close caused them to drop the litter and hit the ground. It showered us with rocks and mud, some of it landing on my face. We finally arrived at the aid station just in time for them to slide my litter into the back of an ambulance which was ready to depart for a field hospital. I really felt guilty being treated so royally with what I considered to be so small a wound.

I must have been the least severely hurt of the half-dozen who occupied the bunks in the ambulance. Some of them had attendants and were being treated to intravenous drugs or plasma or both. I can still recall how guilty I felt—and how lucky to be alive.

In short order our ambulance pulled into a community of tents, (similar to what we have now seen in the T.V. series, *M*A*S*H*.). I was given a tetanus shot and as I was shaking uncontrollably was covered with some warm blankets and given something strong to drink which I assumed was first rate Scotch. Activity in that M.A.S.H. unit was like a scene from hell. The stream of broken bodies being brought in never seemed to end. The aprons of the staff looked like those worn by workers on the line in an abattoir.

My severe shaking and teeth chattering continued for the better part of three days and I was becoming concerned that I would be like that for the rest of my life. My jaws ached from the clenching of my teeth every time a shell had landed close. Because of the soupy mixture of phosphorous and mud my head received on the mountain the skin all peeled from my face, ears and neck. I was still prying the stuff from inside my nasal cavities several days later. To add insult to injury as far as my nerves were concerned, the M.A.S.H. unit was located close to a very busy road leading into the mountains. The heavy trucks coming down or going up the steep grade were continually shifting gears and the sound easily translated in my state to that of incoming shells. I spent three days in tent city before it was my turn to be shipped out.

Fortunately, by the time I was loaded onto a hospital train for the trip to Naples my nerves had calmed down considerably. Enroute our train was strafed by a lone enemy aircraft. It was a rude interruption as there were casualties on the train which included the already wounded and some of the nurses. The train had red crosses on its roof.

On arrival in Naples, I and others were transferred by ambulance to the 17th American General Army Hospital. It was hard to imagine that such a facility would then still exist in the otherwise war-damaged city of Naples. For an infantryman just out of the mud, rain and shellfire of the mountains, that place was Heaven. The 17th was one of three modern four-story buildings atop a beautiful height of ground surrounded by groves of umbrella pines and overlooking one of this world's most spectacular views. To our southeast about fifteen miles distant was the massive cone of Vesuvius. Directly to our south and about the same distance away lay the Isle of Capri, across the Bay of Naples. I was to spend the next 37 days in the luxury of white sheets and warm, clean surroundings.

X-rays revealed that the small piece of shell fragment which had gone right through my left ankle had not damaged any bone. My convalescence was marred by the daily arrival of newly wounded members of my unit with their tales of various battles and of the subsequent loss of many more of my friends and compatriots. I was particularly sorrowed to learn that on Christmas Day my very close companion, Charlie Dawson, who took my place in my absence, was decapitated by a shell which made a direct hit on the rocky outpost which was being used as our battalion headquarters. The same shell killed Captain Miles Cotton, our battalion adjutant and badly wounded Colonel Jack Akehurst.

Christmas Eve of 1943 was one which I shall long remember. I was still in the 17th General and able to walk around with a cane. Early in the evening the Luftwaffe paid a visit to the Naples waterfront where many ships were unloading the tools of war. The air raid caused a lot of destruction. In the harbour area some several miles away huge fires were started by the bombing. Word soon reached us that one fire in particular was nearing a huge ammunition dump and thoughts of the Halifax Explosion of World War I were brought to mind. Reports kept everyone in a state of dread as the fire seemed to be getting closer to the ammo. Tales of bravery of the engineers who were manning the bulldozers and other heavy equipment were being reported by a newsman on the scene.

After what seemed like an eternity of waiting for a tremendous explosion it was announced that the fire had at last been brought under control. (I had practically a first hand account of the Halifax explosion as my mother was living about twenty miles from Halifax when that devastation occurred. In her home they felt the shock wave and heard the blast even at that distance. It was the result of two ships colliding in the harbour starting a fire on the one which was heavily loaded with ammunition to be shipped overseas for the war in France. The ship which was on fire eventually exploded with the largest man-made explosion prior to that of the atom bomb which was dropped on Hiroshima in World War II. At the moment of detonation witnesses reported being able to see the bare rock at the bottom of the harbour. Many persons for miles around were blinded by flying glass as windows were blown out while they watched in horror.) The natural terrain of Naples would have lent itself to an even larger number of casualties had the fire not been contained. Over a million people lived in Naples in 1943.

On or about the 10th of January, 1944, I was discharged from the hospital. I returned to my unit which had been pulled out of the line and was then back in the broken down barracks in Santa Maria di Capua. We spent most of January there resting up and waiting for more walking wounded to be released from the various hospitals. We were also preparing for more action on a front which the generals and politicians were planning to open. Little did we know that it would be known for many months as the "Anzio Beachhead." It was during that period that I almost blew it for sure.

The evening before we were slated to sail up the west coast of Italy to the beaches of Anzio and Nettuno another staff sergeant and myself decided to "go out on the town." The town in question being the small city of Caserta which was only about two miles to our east. It was really just an oversized town and was famous for having a very large palace which was commandeered by the military for the headquarters of the American Fifth Army. All we had in mind was a bit of time in a bar to unwind and keep our minds off the possibilities of being killed tomorrow. A common practice so I've been told. In any event we did have "a few" and as time was getting on we headed back to camp via the blacked-out streets of Caserta.

We hadn't gone too far when I discovered a Jeep which someone had neglected to chain to a lamp post. I suggested to my friend that, being as how my ankle still hurt quite a bit to walk on, we may as well drive back to camp and let the careless driver of the Jeep retrieve it in the morning. We climbed in and I drove off in the direction of the main intersection of the town. We had to pass through it on the way out to our barracks. As we approached the corner I began to loose power in the rear wheels and kept stepping on the gas and shifting the gears around. We had enough forward momentum to wheel past an American M.P. who was on duty at the intersection. We coasted about a half a block past him before our Jeep came to a complete stop. I could see his white helmet bobbing in the rear vision mirror as he jogged in our direction. I realised that we could be in big trouble and told my friend to get lost in the dark while I slipped over into the passenger's seat. The M. P. soon caught up to the Jeep and was demanding to see my "trip ticket," my authority for driving the vehicle. I quickly told him that I had just hitched a ride with a stranger and couldn't figure out why he had taken off so fast. I figured that I had everything under control when out of the darkness ahead I heard the voice of my dumb friend. "Is he giving you a bad time, Cottingham?" How did I ever get mixed up with him?

At that point the M.P. drew his .45 Colt pistol and, waving it in our faces, suggested we both accompany him to his police station. It was just around the corner which we so recently passed. I was later to learn that my "friend" had probably kicked the high and low selection lever of the jeep into a neutral mode in his not quite sober state. Hence the lack of power to our rear wheels. Had I ever driven a jeep before I may have known how to shift it into the proper gear.

When the M.P. took us into his HQ he sat us on a bench near the front door. He instructed the off-duty guys who were playing cards at the far end of the room to keep on eye on us while he went out to find the Provost Marshall who was somewhere out on patrol. When he had been gone less than half a minute we decided that we had better make a run for it if we didn't want to end up in deep doo. We sprang up from the bench together and charged out the front door knocking over the M.P. and his boss who were just coming up the steps. We dived around the corner in the black-out and kept on running as hard as we could. We dove down the first back alley we came to as they had got off a couple of shots in our direction. By that time my left ankle was screaming at me as I was abusing it with every painful step. There was no time for comfort as we dodged through a lot of side streets and back alleys on our way out of Caserta that night. I think my friend had sobered up considerably by the time we made our way into camp and found our sleeping bags. I know I had.

There was a rather humorous incident the following day as our regiment moved out in trucks on our way to Pozzuoli (the birthplace of Sofia Loren). Our convoy of trucks had to proceed through Caserta. As luck would have it the whole column halted for a minute or two just as we passed the now famous corner of the night before. My friend and I were sitting right by the tail gate of our truck. As we surveyed the scene we noted with some consternation that the same M.P. who had taken us in the night before was again on point duty about ten yards away directing traffic. Just as our convoy began to move off he turned in our direction and spotted us. This time we were fully armed ourselves and in the company of a lot of mean looking members of our detachment. He did a double take and broke into a big grin. We gave him a friendly wave as our truck picked up speed. Pozzuoli was the port of embarkation we used as we boarded landing craft for the trip to the Anzio Beachhead. We were given to understand that there would be very little resistance there as the first waves had already gone ashore and were moving inland.

Several hours later we approached the beaches of Anzio-Nettuno, two summer resort towns very close together and about 40 miles south of Rome. There was an aerial engagement going on above our heads. One of our Spitfires was in trouble. There was black smoke streaming out of its engine. As it passed over us the pilot turned it on its back and dropped out safely deploying his parachute. He landed in the sea quite close to us and a patrol boat in the vicinity went over and pulled him out of the water.

Many years later (1962) my last year as C.O. of Neepawa's Air Cadet Squadron, the inspecting officer at our final parade was a Wing Commander by the name of Tony Golab. He was the C.O. of RCAF Stn. Rivers. He was also a former quarterback of the Ottawa Roughriders. I noted that he was wearing the Italy Star and after the parade we were socializing and I asked him what he flew in the Italian Campaign. He replied that he was in "Spits." In further conversation it turned out that he was the one I had seen parachuting into the sea off Anzio. He told me that I was the first person he ever met since that day who had witnessed his spectacular misadventure.

CHAPTER 16

Anzio Beachhead

Shortly after we had gone ashore from our landing craft (LCI) and proceeded inland a couple of hundred yards the port was attacked by several dive bombers. One of them made a direct hit on the landing craft we had just vacated. We did not learn what kind of casualties the crew most likely suffered. Because of my painful ankle still requiring fresh dressings every day I was considered "walking wounded" and was given a special duty by Colonel Marshall, our regimental commander. I was detailed to take a section of men and guard the extreme right corner of what was then to become known as the Anzio Beachhead.

Our mission was to maintain a lookout where the Mussolini Canal flowed into the Mediterranean Sea. There was an old watch tower there which I have referred to ever since as "my castle." It was known as Foce Verde. The remainder of our responsibilities consisted of patrolling a two mile long beach which ran northwest from "my castle" to another old structure which really was a castle, Torre Astura. It could be reached by crossing a short causeway with a drawbridge at its entrance. When the tide was low we could see the foundations of a much larger edifice which the locals told us was the foundation of Nero's villa. He may have played the fiddle there while Rome burned. About half-way between the two points mentioned there was an old villa nestled in the sand dunes which provided a good view of the entire beach. We set up our headquarters there in the beginning of our tour of duty. We soon had phone lines strung to connect us to Regimental HQ. My squad was responsible to Colonel Marshall and acted as the eyes and ears of the right flank of his regiment.

During the first weeks in that location we maintained a beach patrol with our jeep. One night an American submarine reported that there was a tank making its way northward on our beach. It was obvious that their radar had mistakenly zeroed in on our jeep. We were quick to advise our H.Q. to tell them to hold their fire. We never had occasion to find the enemy attempting an "end run" in small boats but there was plenty of other activity worthy of note.

The American heavy bombers which were stationed on the island of Sardinia made many runs over our position on their way to and from Rome where they concentrated on the railway yards and other military targets. One day as they were returning from their mission over Rome one of their planes, a B24 Liberator, had a fire in the port inboard engine. We counted eight men bailing out of it while it was still over the land and the ninth managed to bail out as it crossed the coast and was over the sea. Just after he bailed out the fire had weakened the fuselage so badly that it side slipped towards our villa and appeared to be going to fall right on top of us. It burned in two just in time to drop into the sea near our beach. A very exciting moment to say the least. I phoned HQ to have a boat sent out to pick up the airman who was still out in the water.

On another occasion a Heinkel 111 was shot down and crash landed at high speed and at a very shallow angle of approach. As it plowed into the ground the engines both broke free of the wings and came tumbling towards us. One of them finally came to rest about five yards short of our villa. Neither of the crewmen who bailed out had time to deploy their chutes. By some coincidence in going over to examine the wreck we came across a Spitfire which had come down near it. The pilot may have been able to walk away from it as it was in fair condition. It had slid to a stop on soft sandy ground. It must have happened before our time in that area. There was never any shortage of aerial activity over the Anzio Beachhead. Coupled with the almost never ending attempts of the enemy to drive us all back into the sea by attacking here and there it was an experience I shall live with for the rest of my life. We were to spend over one hundred days there.

There was a paved road which ran parallel to the beach about fifty yards inland. It ran from the Mussolini Canal back to the old castle to our northwest. It was bounded by the sand dunes on the south and by a shallow lagoon on the north which was about seventy five yards across. One day my sergeant and I chose to walk to the tower on an inspection tour instead of taking the jeep. As we were returning to our villa a sniper in an abandoned farmhouse across the lagoon began to try to cut us down. We were good targets as we strolled along thinking we were safely behind our own lines. Neither one of us was carrying any weapons other than our pistols as we dived into the ditch to our left. For a while he kept us pinned down by knocking sand down around our ears with his shots.

We couldn't stay there all day so we decided to make a dash over the dunes to be out of his sights. Needless to say the one shot he had time to fire as we fled missed us. When we got back to our villa by way of the beach I had a pretty fair idea as to which house he was in. I located it on my map and phoned in the coordinates to one of our supporting artillery batteries. After getting a couple of rounds of smoke close enough to the target I asked them to blanket the area and fire for effect. In no time there was concentrated shell fire which eventually found its target—the farm house. We never did find out if the sniper was dealt with or not. We weren't all that keen to use the paved road after that.

On the 14th of February, 1944, I was still located in the villa near the beach. It was Valentine's Day. It is engraved in my memory as on that day I received a letter from my parents telling me that my brother, David, had been killed. He was a platoon commander in the Loyal Edmonton Regiment. They were involved in the battle for Ortona on the east coast of Italy. I had been expecting such news as my brother had been so good at writing to keep me informed of his travels in the Mediterranean campaign. I had ceased getting his welcome letters a month or so before that. Somehow I knew that he no longer existed. Nevertheless the finality of his death came as a great shock. I had no one near me who knew him to share my grief with. It was a very difficult time for me, not to mention how terrible it was for my parents to have received such word.

Several days later I met my good friend "Spud" Wright on my way to regimental HQ on some errand. Spud had just received word that his brother, a Spitfire pilot, had been shot down and killed. It was a great help to us both to have someone to commiserate with. David and I had been very close as brothers. David was killed two days before Christmas in house-to-house fighting. Ortona was about the meanest kind of battle in which an infantryman could find himself. It was close quarter kill-or-be-killed combat. Reports were that David had thrown a grenade into the next room of a house which had been badly damaged by shell fire. It was an attempt to clear the house of its enemy occupants. The detonation of his grenade was all it took to bring the house down on him. When his men dug him out of the rubble he was dead.

Shortly after that we moved our headquarters to the tower on the Mussolini Canal. It turned out to be an even more exciting place than our villa near the beach. We were still responsible for patrolling the beach at night but in addition to that we played host to various artillery forward observer parties for the next month and a half. It also became a famous spot for various news media types who were brave enough to risk getting a good look at the front line. A lot of news releases were datelined from that old tower.

An incident worthy of recall occurred "one dark and stormy night." The one and only time we had a visit from a British firing party it was raining "cats and dogs" and the front was completely quiet. Even the enemy had no stomach for manning his guns in all that rain. The British party consisting of a captain, his jeep driver, his batman and his radio operator drove up to our tower, and with their captain barking orders, unloaded their gear and prepared to settle in for some fire direction. Their heavy guns were, for some reason, moved into a position to support our American sector.

They had hardly been with us for an hour when it became all too apparent to me that the captain was "personna non gratia." He was treating his men like dogs as only certain British officers could do. I suggested to him that as I was in charge in the tower he had better begin to act more humane in respect to his men or he could leave. He huffed and puffed and threatened to have me court-martialled for insubordination. I handed him our phone and suggested he call Colonel Marshall if he was unhappy with his surroundings. He had his men load up all of their gear and they took off into the night. We never saw them again.

Our days and nights in that tower are among the most lasting memories of my wartime experiences. It was the only time, during my five and a half years in the service, that I could personally be located by sticking a pin in a situation map of territory held by the Allied Forces. We were at the extreme right corner of the then famous Anzio Beachhead. A very interesting posting indeed.

We were fortunate not to have suffered any casualties in our tower while my crew and I were stationed there. However, shortly after we vacated the place an artillery officer whom I had come to know was killed as he backed his jeep too far in turning around. He ran it over a mine. We had warned everyone about the mine field which the Germans had planted. The observation post which we ran there was always a tempting target for the enemy's artillery and our very thick walls saved us from their occasional attempts to put us out of business. They became reluctant to fire at us as our spotters were very good at calling for fire on their gun locations whenever they revealed themselves. The American gun batteries in our sector were experts in "blanketing" any target with an intensive barrage which must have been a terror to live through. It helped to make us feel more secure in our outpost.

One morning the enemy chose our sector for a concentrated assault on the Allied front in an attempt to drive us back into the sea. They happened to pick the wrong place for their attack as our lines had quite a bend in them at that point. Their main thrust was allowed to enter what looked to them like a gap in our line. It was instead a trap as they became surrounded on three sides by our machine gunners and mortar people. The whole operation was under observation from our tower. I was able to give the platoon commanders a running commentary over our field phone.

When they had almost reached our lines they were brought under concentrated mortar and machine gun fire from three directions. Our guys in the line had a field day and in short order they had taken about two hundred prisoners. The attack had failed and resulted in severe losses to the enemy. Our people were well dug in and fared much better. The prisoners taken in the attack provided a lot of information about the enemy positions and strengths to our immediate front. That proved to be very useful in formulating plans for the eventual break-out from our beachhead.

The top of our tower was a great spot from which to observe the many air raids which the enemy launched against our port facilities back in Anzio. Often at night they would send over several bombers. The first wave usually lit up the scene by dropping parachute flares. That was followed by bombers with high explosives which were mostly directed at ships which were unloading the vital supplies we needed. Anzio wasn't a real port in the sense as there were no piers for the unloading of deep draft vessels. Supplies were unloaded into shallow draft tenders, mostly DUKWs, which were self-propelled vehicles capable of ferrying supplies to the beach and driving up onto dry land.

A nighttime air raid was, among other things, a very spectacular show to watch from a safe distance. One could be hypnotized by the play of searchlights sweeping the sky and zeroing in on various aircraft. They created a fantastic backdrop for the tracer bullets which appeared to float upwards like strings of red hot beads searching for their targets. It was very seldom that any of those shells found their targets. When they did there was sometimes a ball of fire which once was an aircraft and its crew.

In one very trying period on the beachhead the air raids were so effective that supplies of ammunition and food became critical. There was a distinct shortage of food in particular as ration supplies were disrupted. We discovered that boxes of canned foods and other packaged goods were being washed ashore from ships which had been hit. We were quick to organize salvage parties and supply some of our people that way.

The food shortage led to an event worthy of recall when a party of engineers drove up to our tower in their jeep looking for food. We had accumulated several extra cases of C & K rations from the beach. They offered to trade us their bi-pod mounted Browning .30 cal. belt fed machine gun for a couple of cases of food. We jumped at the deal as we could always use some more weaponry. I had never been checked out on a belt fed machine gun so decided to fire a few rounds out over the sea for practice after they had left. The first thing we noticed was that the bi-pod that the gun was mounted on was part of their jeep and of course left with them.

Without the mounting it was necessary to improvise a way to hold the gun. I chose to wrap the barrel with some heavy paper so the heat of firing would not burn the hand I had to hold it with. I misjudged the heat that firing a couple of bursts would create and had to drop the gun in the sand as I fired the second burst. For some unknown reason the gun continued firing. It bucked around in a circle firing until the whole ammo belt was used up. The firing mechanism must have jammed. It shouldn't have fired after my finger left the trigger. I still can't figure out how it missed hitting any of us as we dove to the ground and scrambled to get out of its lethal path.

Tower on the Mussolini Canal. Water colour by Peter Cottingham.

Photo by Brian Bailey.

On another occasion I was standing on top of our tower with Colonel Marshall viewing the terrain to our east. An enemy bomber appeared from the north heading in our direction and following the line of the Mussolini Canal. It was just after dusk but we could make out the unmistakable silhouette of a Heinkel 111. While we watched there appeared to be a small plane falling away behind it with smoke trailing out its rear. My first reaction was that they must have shot down one of our fighters but I had heard no shots. Colonel Marshall shouted "It's a radio controlled bomb." It had been launched in our direction by the bomber crew but its angle of decent was a little high fortunately. It sailed over our heads about ten feet above us and crashed with a mighty explosion into the sea just off our beach. We were mesmerized by the technology. It was the same kind of bomb they were using against ships in the Mediterranean Sea. They must really have wanted my tower out of action as those bombs cost "an arm and a leg" to make.

After that episode Colonel Marshall decided that the artillery boys could have the "castle" all to themselves. My crew and I were dispersed into the regiment and I went back to my former job as battalion operations sergeant. Our battalion HQ was about two miles inland from the beach and a couple of hundred yards back from the front line.

My former battalion commander, Lt. Colonel Jack Akehurst was now the commander of the second regiment of the Force. Our battalion had a new commanding officer, a Lt. Colonel Walter Grey. Captain Jerry McFadden, who had temporarily taken over after the wounding of Jack Akehurst in the mountains near Cassino, was then second in command of our battalion. We all shared a one-story building at a very busy crossroad.

For a month or so life in Bn. H.Q. was relatively safe and but seldom boring. There was the odd mortar attack which kept us in a state of readiness and sometimes mortal dread. The odd frontal attack which was mounted near our sector was dealt with by our line companies with the support of artillery. Most nights we could hear the extremely large caliber shells fired by "Anzio Annie,"as they whistled overhead on their way to the town of Anzio. That was the nickname given to a railway gun which was mounted on two flat cars and stored in a railway tunnel in the mountains to our east in the daytime. It was capable of throwing a shell which weighed about 560 pounds for a distance of thirty-eight miles. The entrance to its tunnel was often attacked by our dive bombers in the daylight. The gun crew became expert at repairing the tracks and roadbed so that they could haul it out and fire it at night. Our headquarters was directly under its most used trajectory.

One dark night, either by accident or design, two of its shells landed roughly in the middle of our crossroad. The first one to land scared the bejabers out of all of us as we could hear its usual whistle becoming a meaningful scream in our direction. Most of us made it down the stairs into the wine cellar located under our main floor. The explosion of the shell left a crater in the road large enough to bury a three ton truck. Our building was banked with dirt and windows shattered. We had just about decided to go back up the stairs when shell number two came screaming viciously in our direction. Every one of us was sure that we would receive a direct hit. We almost did. The shell landed about ten yards closer to our building throwing a large round rock about the size of an easy chair up onto, and almost through, our flat roof.

We were badly shaken by that one and had heard a lot of commotion up on the main floor. In looking up we could see that our switchboard operator, Tom Schwenke, was still sitting at his switchboard and was covered with lath and plaster. Above his head was the rock with a third of it sticking through the hole it had made in our ceiling. It's a good thing the rest of the lath and plaster had held or Schwenke would have been an ink spot. We hollered at him to get out of there and join us in the cellar. He would have none of it, saying, "Someone has to run the switchboard." I think he was just putting on a "look how brave I am" act. We did manage to move the switchboard to a better location in the room. That was the one and only time that our HQ was a target for the big stuff.

The next morning we surveyed the damage to the street. It appeared that both of the shells must have penetrated the ground about six feet before they exploded. Each of them left a king sized crater and threw an immense amount of dirt and rock over our building and into our smashed windows. We found bits of the shell casings which were lying about. Their thickness and curvature were most impressive. The only guns larger than that were most surely on the largest battleships.

The enemy shelling of various targets on the beachhead resulted in many casualties. It was estimated that during the one hundred days we were there the casualty total added up to over thirty thousand killed. It became a matter of life or death when approaching a crossroad. We always stopped and looked at our watches. If the time was near any part of a quarter hour we would stop and wait. The Wermacht must have had a rule book which called for shelling crossroads every fifteen minutes. It was also not wise to drive too fast and raise dust. Dusty roads often drew shellfire by indicating traffic.

Troops weren't the only casualties. There was a stable about a quarter of a mile to our west which began to smell up our sector whenever the wind drifted from that direction. It got so bad that my C.O. ordered me to take the jeep and go back to see what was stinking up the place worse than normal. I followed my nose and found a stable which had received a direct hit and contained three badly bloated cows chained to their mangers. I reported same to the C.O. He decided that the cows had to be buried.

I had the idea that as we were qualified to use explosives we then had a valid excuse to requisition a case of T.N.T. and some rope. The C.O. went along with that. Anything to get rid of the smell. The next day our case of T.N.T. arrived and we set to work to bury the cows. I took a couple of guys with me and we drove back to the barn. The stench was so bad that we had to cover our faces with wet handkerchiefs. There was no way I was going to reach down into the bloated necks of the cattle to undo their chains. I managed to break the chains with firing my .45 pistol at them. A fairly dangerous procedure as there was no telling where the bullets would ricochet to in the steel and concrete stable.

Prior to tying ropes to the cows for dragging them out of the stable we dug a hole about twenty yards outside the stable door at an angle we figured would be just right for a controlled charge. We placed half of the T.N.T. blocks in the bottom of the hole. Each block was about the size of a pound of butter and had a hole right though the centre of it lengthwise for placing either the detonator or stringing some primacord through it.

We placed an electrically activated detonator in one of the blocks of explosive and strung some field telephone wire from the detonator to our jeep which we had parked about fifty yards away. Getting the guys to hide behind the jeep I then touched the wires to the battery which we had removed from the jeep and placed behind it. There was a tremendous explosion which achieved the result we had hoped for. I was happy to see that I hadn't forgotten all I had been taught about explosives that first winter in Montana. We had a really deep hole with all of the dirt from it in a great pile to one side.

We then managed to tow each of the cows out and by circling the crater jockeyed them into the hole we had blown. They pretty well filled the crater. We then placed the other half of the T.N.T. in a position to blow the dirt back over the cows. Again we witnessed an awesome display of explosive power. The cows were buried. We put the battery back in the jeep and drove back to our H.Q. We smelled so badly that we were sent back to one of the field hospitals for showers and were issued new clothing. What we had been wearing was burned in the hospital's incinerator. It was days before any of us could enjoy a meal without the smell of the dead cows bothering our appetite. It had apparently penetrated our pores and took some time to dissipate. It's no wonder that the men who operated the grave details after battles have had great mental difficulties for years afterwards.

CHAPTER 17

The Breakout from Anzio

S hortly after the "dead cow" episode the Force was pulled back from the front lines and was replaced by an American infantry unit. We were to spend the next week getting ready to spearhead the long awaited break-out through the enemy lines for the push to Rome.

In our move from the crossroads headquarters to the rear assembly area It was my job to supervise the transportation of various items of equipment. Some of the colonel's personal items were to be included as well. One such item was a suspicious looking glass jar containing a clear liquid. It looked enough like pure grain alcohol that we decided to sample it. We determined that it was indeed potable. We imbibed. One of our party must have over done his sampling as when we arrived at our designated bivouac area he was in a state of sublime inebriation.

Almost every square yard of the Anzio beachhead was visible to enemy artillery spotters with powerful glasses up in the hills to our east. They had no doubt witnessed the movement of our unit to the area we then occupied. The area we were in was considered relatively safe from observation as it was in a wadi. A wadi is an area of considerable size which is a good bit below the surrounding ground. Even so it was wise for everyone to dig himself a suitable fox-hole for protection from incoming shellfire. Most of us availed ourselves of that precaution.

As expected, we became the target for a fairly concentrated barrage for several hours that first night. It was during the shelling that

I heard my inebriated friend calling for medical assistance. He had crawled into his sleeping bag on top of the bare ground without having dug himself some protection. He received a nasty wound from a close shell explosion. A piece of shrapnel had sliced through his upper instep. In no time a couple of medics managed to carry him over to their sandbagged aid post. They dressed his wound and sent him off, with several other casualties, to one of the tent hospitals further to our rear.

Unfortunately no place on the beachhead was out of range of the enemy guns. The red crosses painted on the canvas of the hospital tents were no guarantee that they would not become a target. There were more nursing sisters killed on the Anzio beachhead than in any place else in the European Theatre of Operations. Such was the enemy we were opposing.

I managed to visit my friend a couple of days later. He was the next thing to being a nervous wreck. The wards were heavily sandbagged and had received several direct hits since his admission. The only thing that gave him cause for joy was the fact that his wound made him unfit for further military service. I never saw him again but know that he lived to become a husband and father as I read his notice of death in 1994.

Our location in the wadi gave one of our enterprising fellows, a private soldier by the name of Wright, an idea that was seconded by our colonel. He was given a letter of introduction to the colonel of a British Highland regiment several miles to our left. He had heard that the Highlanders had a complete pipe band among their ranks and were also in a bivouac area training for the break-out.

Wright managed to persuade the colonel of the Highlanders to send the complete band to our area for the afternoon prior to our push (hopefully) through the enemy lines. All that afternoon they marched back and forth playing their wild and inspiring music. It was the next best thing to being piped "over the top," as many Highland regiments had been in fighting Britain's battles over the years.

Prior to moving up to the front for the attack, my battalion commander, Lt. Colonel Walter Gray, insisted that he lead his battalion by accompanying the assault platoon of the leading company. Part of my job was the responsibility for the security of the battalion commander at all times. I was shortly to learn that in certain matters he held his own counsel. I tried to convince him that his battalion had a far better chance of accomplishing its mission if he were to live through the first day of battle. He was beyond my persuasion.

Very few memories are as indelibly fixed in my mind as the events of the 23rd of May, 1944. Prior to Zero hour on the 23rd we had moved from our bivouac area back to the front line at a location being held by the American third division. The movement to the front had been accomplished under darkness and without drawing the attention of the defending enemy. At exactly six o'clock local time, following a very concentrated barrage laid down by our artillery, we scrambled out of our hiding place, the bank of a canal which fed into the Mussolini Canal north of our former sector. We were preceded by a squadron of Sherman tanks which fanned out for us to follow in their tracks as closely as possible. They afforded protection from the machine gun fire we faced and also running in their tracks we could be reasonably sure that any anti-personnel mines would have been exploded for us.

Unfortunately the tanks could only provide cover from our direct front. As we approached the enemy lines, which were only a couple of hundred yards from ours, we began to experience the effect of their cross fire. Our comrades were falling all around as the air was alive with the vicious snap of bullets going by our ears. A burst of machine gun bullets caught my colonel in the throat. We all hit the ground and it soon became apparent that he was mortally wounded. I left him in the arms of our assistant operations sergeant, Dante Raponi. I continued on in the direction of the enemy lines. By that time the Germans were giving up and coming out of their positions with their hands high and running toward us.

It was difficult to refrain from firing at them after experiencing the loss of our own people.

In short order we had breached the main line of enemy defenses which had determined our status as a beachhead for so many months. This was done at a great cost to our regiment and the day was not yet over nor was it yet won. It would prove to be the longest day of my life as we proceeded with our diminished numbers in the direction of number seven highway to our north. Meeting sporadic pockets of resistance we worked our way toward our second objective, the highway we were hoping to cut.

By late afternoon we approached highway seven and it appeared we were in for a well mounted counter-attack. We could see the enemy armor coming across a railway overpass just beyond the highway. Their Tiger tanks were beginning to take a terrible toll on our supporting Shermans. Neither the Sherman's armor nor their weaponry were any match for the Tigers. In retrospect it's hard to imagine how the Yanks could have let themselves lag so far behind in weapon development. Ours were designed for the final stages of World War I. It was criminal to pit them against their more modern antagonists. Up to that point most of the seventeen Sherman's, which had been such a big help in the morning, were still with us. A very one-sided tank battle began with a fury. It was a terrible thing to be mixed up in. It is hard to describe fully, the sights and sounds and naked terror of such a battle. Flesh and bone had never felt so helpless and vulnerable as amidst the explosive whiz and clang of such an exchange. We found ourselves cowering stricken while all around there was burning armor, most of it bearing the markings of the U.S.of A. Mechanized gladiators in a hellish melee of fire and steel and noise.

We set up our Bn. H.Q. in a substantial looking farm building from which we hoped to direct our defenses by radio. We sent an officer from the tank corps upstairs with his radio to try to direct his tanks as best he could. Our building had stone walls about two feet thick. It seemed rather secure at first. The tank officer had no sooner stationed himself in the room upstairs when a shell from one of the Tiger tanks made a direct hit on the room. He was horribly wounded and Tommy Cole and I went up to assist him but to no avail. He had already died.

We scurried back down the outside stairs and back into our H.Q. room. We were almost blown out the door we had entered when an armor piercing round blasted through our room. Its impact as it entered filled the room with pulverized rock particles. The only thing visible through the resulting granite fog was the doorway to the outside air. We hastily exited through same. The round which had penetrated the two-foot thick wall had also exited through the opposite wall and lodged itself in one of our remaining Sherman tanks. It had taken cover behind the building. It amazed me again how quickly a tank crew can all get out of a burning tank. In our haste to find adequate shelter from the tanks which were bearing down on us we scrambled back down the field to a ditch we remembered from a short time before.

Diving into the ditch we could see that the leading Tiger tank was bypassing our H.Q. building and making its way in our direction. It was a situation of utter confusion and terror as our own armor seemed to have been obliterated. There were burning Sherman tanks everywhere we looked. As the Tiger rumbled toward us the odd person stood up to run back into a field of grain, Anyone attempting to flee that way was immediately gunned down by machine gun fire from the tank. One fellow about five or six yards to my right had apparently stowed some white phosphorous grenades in his pack. A bullet from the tank caught one of his grenades and in no time he was burned in two. The sickening sound of his screams and the smell of burning flesh are even now difficult to recall and relate.

As the ground was shaking with the clanking approach of the tank, I looked up into the ashen face of Tommy Cole who was head to head with me in the ditch. I remember saying, "This looks like it,

Tom." He replied, "It sure as Hell does." At that moment the tank in question took a direct hit in a vital spot. It began to burn and we could hear its crew screaming as the ammo it contained began to explode. In very short order there was no more sound except for the flames consuming the tank and its contents. To this day I have no idea what sort of weapon came to our timely defense.

That was the one and only time that I can recall being positive that I was facing certain death. In addition I was somewhat superstitious, which was common to many of us who faced life and death situations on an almost daily basis. The thought was in the back of my consciousness that my dear elder brother, David, was born on May the 23rd. Had fate decreed that his brother, Peter, would depart this world on the same date? David had been killed in the battle for Ortona on the other side of Italy on December the 23rd, 1943, exactly one month after my own birthday.

It soon became apparent that we were being relieved somewhat by an ever increasing stream of fresh troops who had been following in our steps since the breakthrough. It was also obvious that a contingent of tank destroyers had been moved to our sector. They began to take a significant toll on the remaining Tiger tanks. In this they were aided by some aerial support and the cannons of our fighter planes. As we had been badly cut up in our initial assault it was time to rest up and regroup as we still had a lot of territory to cover on the way to Rome.

Word had reached us that the main German defences on the Cassino front to our south had been breached by the Allies at considerable cost. The forces of Canadian, Polish, French and Americans from the south were then making their way north through the Liri Valley to join up with those of us who had been so long on the Anzio Beachhead.

During the morning of May the 24th we managed to cross the highway where we had met so much resistance the afternoon before. I recall the awe with which we surveyed the burned out hulls of the various Tiger tanks which had come so close to halting our advance permanently. A fearsome and monstrous weapon of war. Of course the field was littered with the remains of most of the Shermans we had started out with the day before.

We proceeded northeast to the hill mass which had so long given the enemy the high ground from which to observe our every move. I was scouting ahead with Tom Schwanke, one of our radio operators. We came under fire from an artillery piece somewhere over to our left. We both dived for cover as one shell landed close enough to cover us with dirt. As I hit the ground my left hand landed on what I thought was a live cigarette which Tom had thrown down. I swore at him to be more careful. As it burned into the heel of my hand I scraped it off and discovered that it was a shiny piece of shell fragment from the explosion we dived to shield ourselves from. It was hot enough to adhere to my skin. We determined that it must have been our own artillery so we hastily swung to our right to be more in line with to the direction of our advancing troops. I apologized to Tom.

As we approached Cori it was obvious that the enemy had left for higher ground. The streets of the village were a scene of gross destruction. Burned out vehicles, bloated dead soldiers and horses, tanks and artillery pieces. It was unclear as to which were a result of Allied bombs and artillery or of having been destroyed by the enemy in his haste to leave nothing of value which could be turned against him. In cases where they had run out of fuel or ammunition they often torched their equipment and left it. The German Army used many horses for hauling supplies and artillery pieces. The Italian population of the village were just emerging from a huge cave where they had taken refuge during the bombing and shelling. They appeared relieved to have been "liberated" from the hated Tedeschi in spite of the damage done to their small town.

As the evening of the second day approached we witnessed another terrible tank battle. This time we were on the high ground, almost a mountainous ridge, which we had to traverse on our way from Cori to the town of Artena, our next objective. We were in a relatively safe position to observe the mayhem which was taking place in the valley below us. German tanks had made their way into the valley which ran between the ridge we were on and the Albano Hills to our west.

The enemy tanks were trying to protect the escape route of the column fleeing north in the Liri valley. Our own tanks and tank destroyers were having more success than they had the day prior as their fire appeared to be wrecking havoc on more of the enemy than our side was losing. Again we marveled at the awesome spectacle of those mechanized giants in mortal combat. By the time the sun went down the valley below us was a scene of carnage beyond description with burning tanks and tracer fire and the continual noise of the guns and their deadly impacts. It soon became too dark for picking out targets so the firing stopped and we could hear the engines roaring as the surviving combatants changed positions or withdrew from the field. From all appearances the enemy's second counter attack had fizzled out.

By mid morning of the third day we had reached the outskirts of the town of Artena. We had approached Artena from the ridge south and west of the town. During the night we had managed to get a bit of much-needed sleep. As we "bedded" down under the stars, using our ground sheets to ward off the chill, I managed to have a chat with our new battalion commander, Captain Jerry McFadden. He had assumed command after our loss of Colonel Walter Gray during the break-out. It was during that conversation that "Jerry" told me that there wasn't a bullet with his name on it. I remember thinking at the time, "Who the hell does this guy think he is anyhow?" The remainder of our time in contact with the enemy appeared to prove him quite prophetic. He came through unscathed.

As we approached Artena we came under some heavy fire by some Neblewerfers. They were a six barreled rocket launcher which the enemy had perfected. Its bark was almost worse than its bite as it had organ reeds implanted in its tail fins to create a most frightening noise as it came howling through the air in our direction. With six of them coming in rapid succession it was the most unnerving experience of all to be caught in one of their barrages. They were actually more effective at demoralizing than in the few shrapnel injuries they produced.

After the rocket attack subsided we were treated to some heavy artillery which, when one of their rounds landed fairly close, produced a very rare and strange effect. After a few seconds of listening to what sounded for all the world like a very powerful boomerang circling us at high speed, the object making all the weird noise landed very close to me with a sharp ker-chunk into the side of the hill I was trying to bury my head in. Part of it was sticking out of the mud. I pulled it out and had a good look at it. It turned out to be half of a brass rifling ring from a large caliber shell. I would think that it had broken off during flight or as a result of the shell exploding. Its shape caused it to imitate a very high speed boomerang as it circled around our area so viciously.

During a lull in the action we found what we considered to be a suitable vacant stone house in which to set up our battalion HQ. It was a one room farm house with thick stone walls. We laid out our maps of the area and were plotting out next move when a lone artillery shell hit the roof of our building. There is no way to adequately describe what it is like to be in a room with four or five men when the room receives a direct hit from a high explosive shell. It's bad enough to be in a room when an armour piercing shell passes through it as was the case during the tank battle we were caught in the first day.

The first reaction is that we have been in the middle of a terrific explosion. The concussion, plaster dust and noise are such that our first thoughts are, "How many pieces of shrapnel have gone through me?" We check ourselves over for holes and bleeding because the concussion leaves the impression that we are now human sieves. Realization that I was miraculously in one whole piece allowed me to look around to see how many of my friends have been wounded or even killed. As it happened in that incident our only casualty of note was my friend Tommy Cole. He found to his surprise that he had several holes in his legs where shell fragments had passed through missing all the bones. A miracle.

We bandaged him up and when the shelling abated, shipped him off in our jeep to look for an aid station. He was able to join us about a month or so later. Just in time to get ready for our "Cruise" to the German occupied French Riviera.

Artena and its environs were to prove a very nasty obstacle on our round about route to the Eternal City. The problem was that highway number six, which ran past Artena about a mile to the north, was the main escape route for the considerable remnants of the fleeing enemy forces which were being pushed northwest from the recently breached Cassino front. The enemy was "pulling out all the stops" to keep the highway open for the fleeing troops. They had established a strong point about a half mile north of the town of Artena just south of the village of Valmontone and were protecting it with various infantry who were dug in and with flakwagons and at least a half dozen eighty-eights and some Neblewerfer rocket launchers.

Our mission was to try to cut the highway to Rome to prevent the enemy saving his manpower and equipment to fight another day. Thus it was that we found ourselves in another situation of intense combat. It proved to be costly to our unit in the number of killed and wounded. We did not enter the town of Artena but skirted around the left side of it in a sunken road. We used that road for cover as we prepared to launch an assault on an enemy held ridge between Artena and Valmontone. After a few brief and costly fire fights we managed to gain possession of the ridge. Our battalion HQ was established once again in a farmhouse just short of the top of the ridge but well within mortar range of the entrenched enemy. We were to occupy that farmhouse for the better part of the next three days.

Part of our Third Regiment had managed to occupy the town of Artena which became a target for the eighty-eights near Valmontone. Counter battery fire whistled over our heads for most of the three days we were there causing much destruction in the Artena area. At one point it appeared that the enemy was going to launch an all out assault on our ridge position. They were determined to keep their highway open at all costs.

During the first day and night of our occupation of the farmhouse we received a lot of mortar fire. One of the shells made a direct hit on the edge of our roof. Again it was a miracle that so few people were hurt. One of them was the first sergeant of one of our companies who was just leaving to go up to his company. He had to be evacuated for serious medical treatment. It turned out that his wounds were serious enough to get him a trip home to the States. The other fellow was patched up by our medics and preferred to remain on duty as he wasn't badly wounded

As a result of the constant firing our forward troops had to do with their machine guns ammo for their .30 calibre Brownings was dangerously low. At that point Colonel Marshall, who had now joined our H.Q. as the regimental strength was now down to the size of a couple of companies, asked me to accompany him on a fairly dangerous foray to look for ammo. As it happened there were several Sherman tanks in a "hull down" position to our left flank just below the top of the ridge but able to fire over the crest. They wisely kept their hulls below the ridge top as they were no match for the eighty-eights they were facing. The colonel and I approached the tanks from the rear and hammering on their hulls with our rifles (a kind of shave-and-a-hair-cut code) we were able to get them to open their hatches and hand us some belt fed .30 cal. in steel carrying boxes. We guessed correctly that they wouldn't think we were the enemy. We managed to get four or five boxes of ammo in that manner. We apparently scrounged enough ammo to tide us over until supplies arrived from the rear.

The next evening it was apparent from all the preparations the enemy was making, and the increased intensity of his mortar and artillery fire, that they were planning to push us off the high ground and recapture the ridge to relieve their situation.

Colonel Marshall, had sent for an artillery firing party to come to our HQ and direct some heavy fire onto our position in general. He ordered our company commanders to have all of our people leave their fox holes and retire to the sunken road about a hundred yards to our rear. The position which they had been holding would then be brought under heavy fire by the newly arrived 150 mm's which our supporting artillery had recently acquired.

As we had a wine cellar in our Battalion HQ building we decided to wait out the barrage in the cellar on the chance that none of the shells would hit our building. The artillery party stayed there with us on the understanding we would stay with them in case the enemy had already started to overrun our ridge. It was with mixed feelings of fear and exhilaration that we stayed in that cellar during the heavy concentration of large caliber shells which followed. Miraculously our farmhouse was not hit but some of the shells landed almost too close for comfort. The intense shelling lasted five or six minutes. Our troops had orders to return to their positions on the ridge as soon as the firing stopped. It was a well executed manoeuvre. The enemy was in complete disarray and badly mauled by the barrage. It had saved the day for us. There were no further attempts to take our ridge positions.

A couple of days later our positions were occupied by another Allied Unit and we were ordered to head southeast down the Liri Valley to meet up with the Allies which were driving the enemy ahead of them from the south. It turned out that there were only token remnants of the Wermacht left in the valley. We encountered some resistance from machine gunners they had deployed as a rear guard. The resistance was quickly overcome whenever we came across it by our superior firepower and numbers.

We finally reached the outskirts of the town of Colle Ferro at which we came to the entrance of what appeared to be an ammunition dump. It was a huge earthen mound covered by vegetation and had a narrow gauge railway track running into its depths. We cautiously entered it and subsequently found it to be deserted. There was a considerable supply of large calibre artillery shells in various bays into which the tracks ran. There were also stalls for either horses or mules which must have been used for hauling the carts, some of which were still loaded with shells. It seemed like a good place to rest while we awaited further orders. Orders were quick to come to move out as someone had discovered a ticking sound in one of the mangers. The place had been set to be blown sky high.

We entered the town proper and discovered that Allied troops from the south were already in charge and had rounded up some German prisoners. The Anzio Beachhead became history as we were then in contact with the rest of the Allied war effort in Italy. It was a great day for those of us who had spent over one hundred days trying to keep the enemy from driving us back into the sea from whence we came.

It was soon discovered that some of the prisoners were familiar with the time bomb and its life span. It was set to go off in about twenty-four more hours. They were given the choice of defusing the bomb or being locked in the tunnel with it. They chose the former. An explosion of all that ammo could have wiped Colle Ferro from the map.

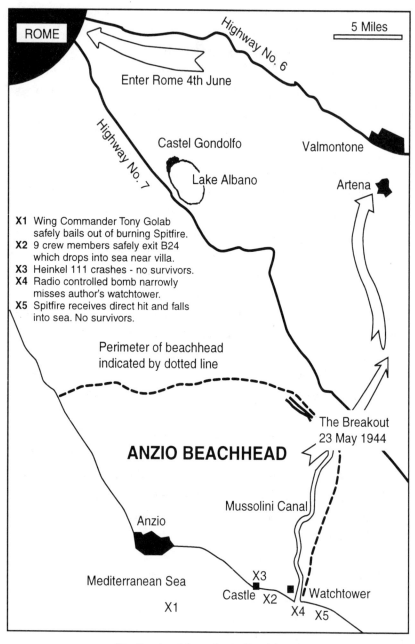

The Breakout from Anzio Beachhead

CHAPTER 18

The Road to Rome

The situation in our sector had changed very quickly as it became evident that enemy resistance had collapsed. We were hastily loaded into the first troop transports we had seen since the night before we had left the beachhead. There was no resistance as our trucks headed first back to Artena and north into the then abandoned town of Valmontone. We were appalled at the damage that our exchange of artillery fire had afflicted on the latter. As night approached we swung westward onto the highway that led to Rome. Our convoy of trucks must have been preceded by a fast tank or two with road clearing equipment as we began to see the results of our superior air power. Both sides of the highway were littered for mile after mile with burned and wrecked enemy equipment, weapons, vehicles, dead men and horses.

While we were congratulating ourselves on perhaps being on the winning side for a change we were rudely awakened by a deadly display of tracer bullets strafing our highway by a low flying aircraft coming from the west. Our driver quickly jammed on the brakes as we all jumped out of the truck and made for the fields beside the road. It was impossible to estimate the damage done to our convoy in the dark but our immediate area seemed to have escaped any major damage. There was a strong suspicion that we had received "friendly fire" from one of our own pilots who hadn't been advised of our rapid progress westward.

While still several miles from the gates of Rome our convoy

halted and we had a hastily called candle lit meeting with Colonel Marshall and our company commanders in a roadside room commandeered for that purpose. Col. Marshall was expounding the uniqueness of our venture telling us all that Rome hadn't been conquered from the south since Hannibal. He also made some reference to the fact that before the day ended we might well be either dead heroes or live ones. From the events which followed I am sure that he wanted to be the first Allied Colonel to enter the Eternal City. Little did we know how prophetic his words were to be.

In the confusion which presented itself in the early hours of first light it appeared that more than our colonel had the same idea. In any event we became separated as he claimed some urgency of purpose and left me in charge of a small detachment of our head-quarters staff in what looked like a blacksmith shop. It had a wide open front entrance which opened onto the highway.

While we were watching for the return of Colonel Marshall a lot of our tanks were rushing past and some of our Force personnel had managed to climb aboard them. We decided to head out towards Rome on foot as most of the traffic passing us seemed to be overloaded. Many troops from various regiments were trying to be the first into Rome and appeared to be trying to beat us to that long sought-after goal. We hadn't gone very far when we met an engineering officer who was attached to our unit. He was in shock as he explained that Colonel Marshall had just been killed. He had received a direct hit in the head by one of the random bullets fired by an armoured car which then turned and sped away.

It was quite a blow to all of us and to First Regiment. He was one of the most respected officers in our outfit. His expertise would surely be missed not to mention his strong presence as a leader of men. Losing men like Walter Gray and Alfred Cook Marshall (among many others) was a terrible price to pay for the ground we had gained. Of the six hundred or so of our regiment who left the

Anzio Beachhead on the 23rd of May there were about sixty odd, including myself, who managed to answer the roll call after Rome was finally secured for the Allies on the 4th of June. That was just two days before the more famous "D" Day landings in Normandy.

Some of our people managed to climb onto tanks which were now passing us in greater numbers. As I was still on foot with my squad I didn't manage to get as far forward as the actual fire fights. At least no shots came near me or my men as we made our way into the outskirts of Rome. There were still many sounds of firing and shouts and motor noises but the sources of the gun fire were difficult to ascertain. Pandemonium was the only way to describe the street scenes as we proceeded into the city proper. It was hard to tell who were the friendlies and who may have been the ones to shoot you in the back or from the top of a building.

There were commotions everywhere as some citizens felt brave enough to flush out people who had sided with the Germans while they were in charge. Without knowing the language it was difficult to sort out what was going on. It was best to keep a sharp lookout for any sign of danger to ourselves and let the Romans sort out their own grievances. The majority seemed to be enjoying their liberation.

After several hours it soon became apparent that the city of Rome was pretty well under Allied control. Military Police were already posting "off limits to enlisted men" signs on the better class hotels. We had really no idea where to locate the main body of our unit (if it really still existed) so we managed to find a very good hotel which hadn't been posted. It was great to find that everything in their bathrooms worked. I can't recall how much our suite was or even if we paid for it. I think it was on the house. In any event one night was all we could stay in such luxury and we made the most of the facilities. The next day we learned that remnants of the First Special Service Force were being assembled in a place called Cinecitta which turned out to be a monstrous motion picture lot and buildings near the eastern limits of the city. It was Italy's Hollywood. The army had established the basic requirements of a camp in the film complex and we were housed there for the next night.

The following day we were trucked out to a bivouac area on the beautiful shores of Lago Albano. Lake Albano was at the bottom of huge bowl, in the Alban Hills. It was an extinct volcano crater about ten miles east of Rome. The gentle inner slopes of the natural bowl were rich in vegetation—orchards of cherries, oranges and a few olive groves. The lake was about three miles across and was a great place for swimming. We all swam there in the buff, scarcely drawing a glance from the many overweight women who washed their clothes by beating them against the rocks on the shore. The predominant landmark which overlooked that beautiful scene was the Pope's summer palace. It perched on the northwest rim of the crater in a village by the name of Castel Gondolfo.

During the several weeks we spent in that idyllic setting we mourned our losses, cleaned our equipment and clothing, and generally rested up from the rigors of battle. Some of the more enterprising created some marvelous cocktails from pure medicinal alcohol and various fruits available from the natives. Some were given medals for outstanding bravery and many who had been wounded out during the fighting were slowly returning from their various hospitals. It was always great to see someone that you had feared was among the dead. There were some happy reunions.

During that period I was among the fortunate who managed to get one of the very scarce tickets to the "Army Show" which had come to Rome. It was an all male cast in a show written entirely by Irving Berlin. The revue was in the best theatre in Rome and lasted about an hour and a half. At the end of the show I shall never forget the wave of nostalgia that swept the audience when Irving Berlin in person appeared on the stage and sang his all time best seller—"White Christmas."

We were shortly to learn that our Force Commander, Brigadier General Robert T. Frederick, was leaving to take command of the

First Airborne Task Force. It was being trained for the invasion of Southern France. General Frederick was one of the most often wounded members of our Force. I believe he was wounded slightly on two separate occasions during our entry into Rome but not severely enough to be hospitalized. None of his many wounds put him out of action for very long. Although he looked like a well groomed corporate lawyer he was always at or near the front lines and never far from the fray when the action was hottest. It would be difficult to imagine a more suitably flamboyant character to lead such a Force as ours.

We had an informal parade on the shore of Lago Albano where Gen. Frederick spoke to us in a very emotional farewell address and presented a few more medals to some of the late returnees from hospital. He emphasized the point that you had to be quite exceptional to merit a medal in our outfit. He then stood and shook hands with each of us as we passed by and had many personal comments to those he knew by name.

The commander of our Third Regiment, a Colonel Edwin A. Walker, was chosen to lead the Force for the remainder of our wartime exploits. He had a tough act to follow in Frederick. I think he did quite well but he never earned the respect that General Frederick had. He was a real loner.

CHAPTER 19

A Well Earned Rest

Following our farewell to General Frederick we were ordered to move again. This time we were trucked to the port of Anzio and loaded onto another Liberty Ship, the U.S.S. Cropper. That night we sailed south to the port of Salerno, about twenty miles south of Naples. There we loaded onto a train for a fairly short trip to Santa Maria di Castelabate, a beautiful little fishing village on the shores of the Tyrrhenian Sea.

Santa Maria di Castelabate was to be our base for the next month or two as we again trained in the use of rubber boats for the landings in Southern France. Many of our number were replacements who had not experienced our Pacific Adventure of the year before. It was a fairly restful time as we spent many hours swimming in the clear warm water just off our beach. We lived in pup tents which were scattered throughout the well-groomed grounds of a palace which had belonged to some countess. She was not too happy with our incursion into her private fiefdom, but hey, *"C'est la guerre."* We had been issued rubber boats for training and eventual use in the forthcoming operation and spent many hours becoming familiar with them in the surf.

One day the surf was exceptionally high. It became quite a challenge to paddle out past where the swells of the open sea became the first curling surflike waves as they built up on their way towards the beach. Some of the waves became the huge concave walls of clear green water which surfers prefer in starting their runs towards the shoreline. It was exhilarating to be out there trying to gain the open sea beyond the combers.

During that exercise we usually went out with about four men to a boat. We all wore swim trunks and for my part I had a towel around my neck and shoulders in hopes of avoiding sun burn. Our team had almost succeeded in cresting the final huge wave as we neared the open sea when our boat was flipped over by the force of a gigantic wave. We were thrown out and down with force. I recall that the sandy bottom was very close to the surface even though were were about sixty yards from the beach. The force of the wave shoved my face into the sand as I slid along for several yards.

I surfaced hoping for some air but the towel had become tightly wrapped around my head. I had just started to remove it when another wave hit and shoved me under again. I managed to get rid of the towel on my up the next time and recall almost choking on sea water before I could get my breath. I began to swim towards the shore and soon discovered that by doing so the undertow was taking me backwards more than I could gain on it. The noise of the surf was such that it was impossible to get the attention of the guys who had managed to grab hold of our rubber boat. They had drifted some distance and were busily trying to right it.

I continued to fight the undertow until I was almost totally exhausted. I decided to lie flat and float while the tons of water which had been thrown up in the shallows were rushing back to the sea under me. I waited for the next big wave and swam with it, resting and floating between waves. I soon discovered that the undertow didn't have the same power to drag me backwards when I floated flat as it did when my arms and legs were down lower as I tried to swim against the current.

Using my newly discovered technique I was eventually able to reach the shore in a completely exhausted state. I guess I was fortunate as I later learned that one of our people had drowned in the undertow that afternoon. When I stood up to walk I discovered that

I had a very sore small toe on my left foot. I remembered that it had been caught in the lifeline which ran around the outside edge of our rubber boat. My toe had been broken when we were thrown from the boat, as subsequent X-rays were to reveal. I was shipped out to a field hospital for a week's rest and the toe had a chance to mend in plenty of time for the landing operations in Southern France.

When I was released from the hospital I managed to get a pass and a jeep for a trip to Naples to visit some of our members who were in hospital there. In travelling from Santa Maria di Castelabate to Naples a person takes a route which most people would give their eye teeth to see in this lifetime. Part of the journey is known world wide as the "Amalfi Drive" which skirts the sea on a high corniche overlooking the Bay of Salerno and the Isle of Capri. We also drove through the excavated ruins of Pompeii and Herculaeneum both of which are beneath the frowning mass of the ever-threatening Mount Vesuvius.

Mention of Vesuvius reminds me that while I was recovering from my slight gunshot wound in the hospital overlooking the Bay of Naples old Vesuvius began to put on a show. Every night we could see a short orange red river of molten lava extending several hundred yards down the north slope from the crater at its summit. In the daytime copious quantities of steam could be seen emitting from its cone as well. Later in the winter when we were on the Anzio Beachhead it finally blew its stack with an actual eruption. The results were not nearly as devastating as the one which buried Pompeii and Herculaeneum almost two thousand years ago. However, a lot of ash rained down on the surrounding countryside covering many square miles of vineyards, olive groves, towns and villages. When it blew I was in the tower by the Mussolini Canal. Although we were far away from the scene of eruption we felt the shock wave which rippled through the country. Our tower rocked gently for several seconds. We learned the next day that Vesuvius had erupted at precisely that time.

Just prior to our leaving Italy for the invasion of South of France our Force Commander received the following from Headquarters Fifth Army, A.P.O. 464, U.S. Army Italy:

Subject: *Letter of Farewell*
To: *Commanding Officer, 1st Special Service Force*

1. *It is with deepest regret that I see the 1st Special Service Force leave the fold of the Fifth Army. In this campaign your Force has more than lived up to our expectations at the time of its arrival, although its reputation acquired in the Aleutians had preceded it and great things indeed had been expected.*

2. *The part played by your elite American-Canadian Force is so well known that it hardly needs to be rehearsed at this time. The grueling fighting which you went through on the main front in the dead of winter, the important part which you took in the establishment and in the defense of the beachhead during its historic four months siege, the way in which your relatively small Force maintained an aggressive offensive on a front equal to that held by any full division, and finally your brilliant performance in the final breakout and in the stern fighting which culminated in the capture of Rome have entered history and forged a bright new link in our military tradition.*

3. *I was particularly happy to have under my command your Force with its international composition. Successfully solving the various difficulties which are inherent under such circumstances, your Force symbolizes the efforts of the United Nations in this war, and gives promise for the more solid and permanent peace to follow.*

4. At this time I wish to extend my sincere congratulations for a job superbly executed and my heartfelt best wishes for continued success in your future undertakings.

> MARK W.CLARK Lt. General
> Commanding.

CHAPTER 20

The South of France

A s a prelude to our amphibious operation in Southern France we were given a mission which could be danger-ous but turned out to be a "piece of cake." We loaded our rubber boats onto a destroyer similar in every respect to the Kane that we had used in the Pacific. It was called the U.S.S. Rogers. About the tenth of August we sailed out past the Isle of Capri and northward to the Isola di Ponza, a small outpost Island about sixty miles south of Anzio. It had been occupied by the Germans as a weather station and possibly as an early warning post against sur-prises from Allied aircraft or ships.

True to form, upon reaching our destination, we launched our boats and paddled ashore during a very dark night. Landing in the surf on such a rocky shore was a very tricky operation but we man-aged without too many bruises. Again I witnessed the nervous reac-tion and apparent disregard for safety in the way our members pro-ceeded to let their weapons clatter noisily on the rocks and empty their bladders. A quick sweep of the island and its few buildings indicated that the enemy had not manned it for several days or weeks. The operation did, however, give us some indication as to the time frame we would be dealing with in a similar move against the islands guarding the shores of southern France.

Half a week later we sailed out of Santa Maria di Castelabate on another ship similar to the Kane and Rogers. It was the U.S.S. Tattnall also equipped for ship-to-shore landings. We sailed in convoy with several other destroyers and a couple of Canadian troop ships. En route to our ultimate destination we put in at Propriano Bay on the Island of Corsica to "stretch our legs." We went ashore and bivouacked there overnight and half of the next day.

Propriano Bay was a beautiful place in which to relax. Our bivouac area was just a short walk from a wide sandy beach which would make an excellent site for a resort for the "rich and famous." Instead it was practically devoid of any habitation whatever and thereby obviated the need for bathing suits as we cavorted in the warm azure waters of the bay. The ships, on which we were to continue our voyage to France, were all anchored in the bay about a mile off shore. While I was swimming one of my friends suggested that we swim out to a certain Canadian ship, the H.M.C.S. Prince Henry. It was a liner which in peacetime had operated out of Vancouver for trips to Alaska. My friend suggested that in all probability someone on board might hand us a Canadian beer for being such enterprising fellows as to swim out there for a visit. I really didn't care that much about drinking a beer while soaking wet and naked but decided to accompany him on his swim anyway.

It is difficult to judge distances over water so I really had no idea how far the Prince Henry was from our spot on the beach. After swimming for what seemed like an hour or more I glanced at the ship and noticed that the men standing on its deck looked rather small for a ship that close. I then glanced back at the beach and was shocked to see that the guys on the beach looked equally as small. I experienced a brief moment of major concern as I sized up my position relative to my ability as a "swimmer." It sure focuses a guy's attention when he is faced with a somewhat dicey situation. There was no way I was going to tell my partner that I didn't think I could make it out to the ship. My mind was telling me to do an about face and try not to drown myself at such a tender age. In short order my adrenaline was flowing like it had seldom flowed before and I soon felt almost invincible. I guess I told myself to "shut up and keep swimming." In retrospect I can understand that decisions like that can have fatal results.

It may have taken us another three-quarters of an hour to reach the ship at which time I was completely exhausted. My friend, who appeared to be in much better shape than I, reached for the ship's ladder and attempted to climb up the several stories to the deck. An officer, who had been watching our progress for some time, leaned over the railing and said, "You can't come aboard this ship." We tried to convince him that we were completely exhausted and would like a place to rest before attempting the swim back to shore. He was not impressed and suggested that we hang on to the ship's ladder until we felt sufficiently recovered to return the way we had come.

After taking advantage of his nautical hospitality for about ten minutes our anger gave us renewed strength and resolve. Exhaustion was no longer a factor in our decision to head back to shore. With the wind and the tide now in our favor we had far less difficulty in returning to the beach. It was in towelling myself off that I realised again what a foolish endeavor I had just participated in. It being almost noon and with the sun being almost directly overhead and with the magnifying properties of clear sea water I began to feel the effects of the world class sunburn I had just acquired.

I was in for an even more painful experience later that day as we donned our equipment for boarding our ship for the final leg of the trip to Southern France. The straps of my pack and the webbing of my ammunition bandoliers gave me some indication as to how the galley slaves must have felt under the lashes of their masters. After boarding our ship I was able to obtain some relief by removing my equipment but the damage done to my back was to remind me of my foolishness for a painful week or two.

August the 14th, 1944 was to be an almost identical operation to the one we had performed half-a-world away in the Aleutian Islands exactly a year to the hour before. Even the ship we sailed on (the U.S.S. Tattnall) was identical in every respect to the U.S.S.

Kane of our Pacific experience. Those ships had seen service in World War I as escort destroyers. In that war they had four stacks (funnels) as they were driven by coal-fired boilers making steam for their turbines. They now had more compact oil burning boilers which allowed for a lot of below deck space for troop compartments. They now had only two stacks and a lot more deck space which we used for storing our inflated rubber assault boats. They were now classed as A.P.D's. (Assault Personnel Destroyers.)

We sailed out of Propriano Bay that evening and our convoy proceeded on a steady northwesterly course for the whole of the following day.

At the time my weapon of choice was the M1 Garand .30 cal. semi-automatic rifle. It was considered state-of-the-art weaponry. A very effective piece indeed. I managed to qualify as an expert on it during range firing in Montana. However, its proper maintenance was one of my procrastinations. As it had seen some service during the final days of our Italian Campaign I figured I would never have a better opportunity to clean and oil it than on this leisurely cruise to France.

Sitting on the steel deck of our destroyer I spread out my ground sheet and proceeded to "strip it down," which is army talk for reducing it to its basic parts. As I was cleaning its bolt it occurred to me that the firing pin should probably be removed and oiled. I had temporarily forgotten one of the early lectures I had attended on the care and handling of the M1.

As I nearly completed servicing my weapon I again considered the firing pin and the possibility that it too should be cleaned. So I worked at removing the retaining pin which secured it in the bolt. As the retaining pin was finally dislodged I narrowly escaped being hit in the eye by the firing pin as it whizzed past my head and into the sea. It was then that I recalled that the pin was only to be removed by an armourer who had the training and equipment to do so safely. I then had a harmless rifle, as far as the enemy was concerned. No firing pin, no fire.

I consoled myself with the fact that I still had a .45 cal. pistol and a combat knife so wasn't completely unarmed for the mission at hand. I expected that someone near me would likely be killed or wounded and his weapon would become available. As things were we hoped to be able to accomplish our first objective without firing a shot. Surprise was supposed to be on our side. I put my rifle back together and intended to abandon it for a better one at the first opportunity.

We spent the final hours of daylight going over our plans and rehearsing in small groups as to how we would time our approaches to the various landing spots, climb the cliffs and spread out to our given objectives. About midnight we could see the rotating beacon of a lighthouse on the island to the east of our intended target. The Isle de Port Cros, being in almost complete darkness, loomed as a menacing silhouette directly to the front of our ship at about three or four miles distant. Our moment of truth was fast approaching as our destroyer slowed to a crawl. We prepared to get our rubber boats ready for launching over its sides.

Zero hour was somewhere near three o'clock in the morning at which time we were all loaded into our allotted boats and ready to set off for the enemy shore. We didn't expect this operation to be a "dry run" like the one a year ago in the Pacific. There wasn't a chance that this enemy would retreat without a fight. We each hoped that it wouldn't be too costly. As we paddled towards the shoreline in the darkness there were two elements which caused us undue concern. A naval P.T. boat with a very loud engine appeared to be trying to herd us to the shore as if we didn't know where it was. The noise it made was most unwelcome. I can't imagine who gave them such dumb orders. Stealth and surprise were our most important weapons in any rubber boat landing. Our other cause for concern was the sweeping beam of the lighthouse at the eastern end of the other island.

As we neared the shore and our eyes became accustomed to the darkness we could make out the rocks and trees at the top of the cliff we were soon to climb. We wondered just how close we could get before the enemy would open up with his machine guns and sink us all. A very tense few moments enveloped us as we closed the last few yards to the rocky shore. In questioning the prisoners we later took they did not think it possible for anyone to climb the cliffs where we had chosen to land. Our notoriety for cliff climbing had fortunately not yet been communicated to that island and its defenders.

As we disembarked from our boats amid the rocks the guys again displayed their complete disdain for extra quietness. Almost to a man they let their weapons clatter among the rocks as they proceeded to empty their bladders as the first order of business. It was very reassuring to know that I was still surrounded by a bunch of people with that much confidence in their ability to carry out a dangerous mission. Maybe no one wanted to wet his pants when the shooting started.

After sorting ourselves out by squads, and sections we made our way up the cliff without a great deal of difficulty. There were plenty of hand and foot holds and some sturdy trees here and there growing out of cracks in the rocky face of the cliff. Once at the top we had some difficulty getting through the dense growth of scrub trees. We soon found ourselves on the road which led up to our main objective, the Fortin de la Vigie. It was the fort on the highest point on the island. Thus far we had no indication that the enemy knew of our presence. On approaching the fort we saw no sign of life so we rushed in over a bridge-like ramp which spanned a dry moat.

We were able to get into the compound without firing a shot. A sleepy looking sentry was quite surprised to see us. Unfortunately some trigger happy guy in our party got off a shot in his direction, wounding him and awakening the whole island much to our concern. Our idiot "friend" was to cost us in many ways. He should have stayed back in Italy. A couple of enemy soldiers came rushing out of their quarters carrying a machine gun. In their surprise at seeing so many of us they threw it down and jumped over a low part in the wall of the compound and headed for the woods. Someone in our party gunned them down before they reached the woods. The rest of the garrison, about eight men, came out with their hands held high in surrender and were taken prisoner. We had control of our first objective without losing any of our own people.

Unfortunately we were too hasty in sending our prisoners off under escort to be ferried out to one of the ships standing off-shore. After they had gone we discovered that we had a phone which connected with other forts on the island. As other units of our Force were dispersed to their own targets, the two other forts and a chateau, we learned too late that we may have been able to save them some trouble by communicating with the enemy by phone. We may have been able to convince them all to surrender had we kept our prisoners to talk to them.

As it was we had our interpreter, a Jewish kid from the Bronx, contact the commander of the largest and most impregnable objective, the Fort de l'Eminence, by telephone. We soon learned that we were dealing with a hard nosed Gestapo type who had no notion of surrendering. He was convinced that we did not take prisoners. Another reason we should have kept the prisoners we had to help prove that we did not kill our captives.

In the meantime we found that we had no communication with the third fort, Fort de Lestissac, which was at the west end of the island. It was decided to take the latter by a direct frontal assault through its main gate.What a dumb decision that was as neither of the two forts left could possibly harm the overall operation of the landings in Southern France as it turned out. They were strictly garrisons and sleeping quarters for the troops who manned the big guns which were already under our control. We could have starved them out. The task of storming Fort de Lestissac was given to 3rd Company of our 1st Regiment. It wasn't worth the four good men we lost in taking it. One in particular was my very good friend, Bill Harry from Prince Albert, Saskatchewan. He and I been together since we both took the same parachute course in Britain in 1942. He never got to meet his infant son who had been born shortly after we left for the Italian campaign.

As the commander of the Fort de l'Eminence refused to give up it was decided to give him a demonstration of firepower courtesy of an American aircraft carrier. After communicating our needs to the navy everything was arranged within an hour and a half. We had a ring-side seat for the show which was about to begin.

The sun was high in the southeastern sky as the first wave of dive bombers appeared to materialize from it. Attacks from dive bombers usually came with the sun in their backs as it made it more difficult for ground defenses to spot them. We were standing on the parapet of our captured fort with a good view of the Fort de L'Eminence, just over a mile northwest of us and about one hundred and fifty feet lower, down in the valley.

My first glimpse of the bombers gave us a real jolt as they appeared to be headed directly for our fort. We had heard enough tales of our air support being confused with their targets and wreaking terrible havoc on friendly positions. As the leader of the first wave opened up his cannons it became clear that he had the right target. All of his opening burst went well over our heads, impacting on the fort below us.

After the first wave of four planes dropped their bombs on or near the fort, so much dust and smoke rose into the air that it was impossible for the following waves to hit the target with any degree of accuracy. Some of their bombs actually dropped into the sea on the other side of the target. When the smoke and dust settled we expected to see a white flag raised or at least we expected a phone call to tell of their surrender. Such was not to be.

By then we had some very high ranking American Naval people with us who had come ashore to watch the show from our vantage point. They must have been assured they would be quite safe. They would be able to tell their grandchildren about how brave they were during the South of France landing operations. Discussions with our Colonel Akehurst led them to concur with a new course of action which could produce the desired result. It was decided to call upon our Allies, the British Navy, who happened to have a large battleship, the H.M.S. Ramillies, in the area. We weren't long in getting their cooperation.

The battleship manoeuvred into position within the hour and began to hammer our target with shells from its fifteen inch guns. Previous to that the American cruiser, Augusta, had fired a number of five inch shells at it which had no effect. The walls of the fort were over twelve feet of rock and concrete in thickness. After ten or twelve rounds from the Ramillies a white flag was noticed through the dust and smoke. Firing ceased and the fort began to empty of its defenders as they came out with their hands held high.

When the island had been completely secured we were loaded onto an LCI for transfer to the mainland. A company of French infantry had arrived to protect an air warning station which had already been established on the island. That night our LCI (Landing Craft Infantry) an all steel ship about one hundred and fifty feet in length, was anchored about a mile off shore near San Raphael, a resort town on the Riviera.

About midnight the most vicious thunder storm I have ever experienced struck with a vengeance. Our ship was overloaded with people waiting to go ashore in the morning so most of us had to cower in the rain on the steel deck with no cover from the elements and wait for it to blow over. I had never seen such lightning and to add to its effects some of the ships anchored near us had barrage balloons tethered above them to ward off dive bombers. The odd lightning bolt managed to hit some of the balloons bringing them down in flames. There was always the possibility that one of them might land on the deck of a ship. It was just what our war weary nerves needed.

The next morning we went ashore onto a beach which had been occupied by Allied forces for several days. I had managed to pick up a Thompson sub-machine gun from a chap who had been wounded out the day before we left the island. I again had a weapon in good working order and would carry the "Tommy Gun" for the remainder of my days in the Force.

We experienced an exhilaration unlike that of any previous campaigns as we made our way through some exotic scenery and met people who were genuinely happy to be liberated from their German masters. The euphoria was tempered at the most unexpected times by the wounding and sometimes the loss of some of our men. There were pockets of resistance wherever the enemy chose to mount a delaying action. There was no doubt that they were steadily withdrawing from the Riviera as they realised they were badly outnumbered, but they still chose to inflict casualties whenever possible.

Mines in particular were a constant danger. They had sown a lot of them, especially in paths that troops might use in their pursuit. The kind they were using which were most effective were "shoe" mines, a charge in a wooden box about the size and shape of a pound of butter. Being wood encased they could not be detected by a mine detector. Any likely place on a gravel road could also have mines designed to explode under the weight of a heavy vehicle. One such mine killed the fellow I had swum out to the ship with in the bay at Corsica. He was a medic by the name of George Durham. His jeep ran over a Teller mine.

It was also along this part of the campaign that my very good friend Al "Spud" Wright was cowardly gunned down by a surrendering German officer. The officer lived about two seconds after shooting Spud. Spud appeared to have been killed as the bullet entered his head right beside his left eye and exited from the back of his skull. His men determined that he was still alive so he was taken to the nearest mobile field hospital. From there he was hustled out to a hospital ship. The medical people did a remarkable job in saving his life as he survived the voyage back to Italy and transfer to the Canadian Army Hospital in Caserta. He eventually gained consciousness after several weeks in a coma.

None of us who knew him and learned of his wound ever expected to see him again. I am happy to say that Spud has attended many of our annual reunions and has steadily improved in his mental abilities over the years. He has been one of the favorites of all the people in the FSSF and is always accorded VIP treatment. (Muriel and I had the pleasure of his company at our very last reunion in Helena, Montana in 1992.)

On our progress through the pine forests north of Cannes expecting to meet the enemy at any time I was startled by a very strange incident. Two rough looking civilians came running down a hill from our left flank and the foremost one came right at me with his huge arms wide open. He grabbed me in a bear hug and gave me a big whiskery kiss right on the mouth. He was either awfully hard up for someone to kiss or awfully glad to be "liberated." I recovered from shock as we listened to his tale. In his broken English he related how the two of them managed to escape from the Germans. They were Russian prisoners of war who had been captured on the eastern front and were making their way across France to Spain where they hoped to be interned. Years later as I watched Nikita Kruschev kiss Yuri Gagarin in a like manner on TV I recalled how much "my friend" had resembled Kruschev.

Shortly after I was assaulted in such a friendly manner by the Kruschev look-alike we came out of the pine forest and were held up by some very unfriendly fire. An armoured car guarding the approaches to the small city of Grasse was spraying our area with machine gun fire. In the confusion of deploying and scattering our troops a couple of our people received minor wounds. We soon contacted our cannon platoon and one of their armored half-tracks came to our aid by firing at the armored car with their 75 MM high explosive shells. The armored car made a hasty exit from the scene.

As we entered Grasse without any further resistance we were met by many happy townspeople who advised us that "Le Bosche a parti." Everyone was in a holiday mood knowing that they had seen the last of the conquering "supermen" they had taken orders from for the past two or three years. During a break in the action in Grasse we were invited to rest in the garden of a villa owned by a family from Nice. They were the Seasals. Our headquarters detachment posed for snapshots. The niece of one of France's more famous architects was the one who took the pictures and gave me the address of her family apartment in Nice. We could have prints later when they were developed if any of us got back to Nice after its liberation. Her name was Paule Seasal. The picture of me standing in front of their villa is on the front cover of this saga.

During the drive towards Nice some of our people became casualties as a result of small arms fire and the occasional artillery barrage. But the meanest of all were the mines. Again the majority of them appeared to be the wooden undetectable type. Stepping on ground in which one of them had been lightly buried usually resulted in at least one foot being blown off and sometimes more serious wounds as well.

About two days east of Grasse our headquarters stopped in the grounds of a chateau belonging to E. Philips Oppenheim. It was outside the village of Roquefort-les-pins. The chateau at the time was occupied by a Monsieur Poteau and his family. We enjoyed the hospitality of M. Poteau and took advantage of his offer to use all of his indoor plumbing facilities. The hot bath was a real treat, and I may add, long overdue. The whole of our frontal patrols were convinced that the enemy was indeed in rapid retreat. We still encountered enough of their artillery delaying actions and concerns with mines to keep us in a state of combat readiness and apprehension. Our mission was still to drive them out of Southern France.

From Roquefort-les-pins we had to make a foray into the village of Saint Paul de Vence. I was on a scouting party of about ten men as we entered that village. It was beginning to look as if the local underground forces, anticipating our advance, were taking matters into their own hands and forcing the enemy from their villages and towns without fear of reprisals. We didn't meet any resistance in entering the town, just happy people who were so very glad to welcome us as liberators. (Muriel and I had the privilege of visiting Ste. Paul de Vence in 1994 and were happy to see the name of the First Special Service Force engraved at their northern gate and listed as the liberators fifty years earlier.)

We then passed through the village of Villeneuve-Loubet which had been liberated with a fierce fire fight by our second regiment the previous night. There was a classic centuries old chateau at the top of a small mountain which overlooked the village. It was the property of le Marquis Henri de Pannise-Passis. It had been in his family for over four hundred years. It looked more like a castle to us as it had crenelated parapets, a moat, a portcullis, a drawbridge, a central keep and a tower.

On a trip through southern France in 1994 with my wife, Muriel, we stayed overnight in a motel near Grasse. A friend of mine from the Force told me that if ever I was back in that part of the world I should try to visit the Marquis in his castle. I phoned him from our motel about nine in the morning and managed a conversation with him although his English was not much better than my French. When I suggested that we would like to visit him he replied, "I'm busy." I was willing to forget about the visit when he added, "Eleven o'clock." We drove the ten miles or so to Villeneuve-Loubet and just before eleven I asked a policeman how to get up to the chateau. He gave me excellent directions and we arrived at the gate at about the right time.

There was a ten foot high wall around the entire acreage which contained his castle. A large metal gate barring our entrance had a speaker phone embedded in the wall near it. I pressed the button and the Marquis responded so I announced who I was. He then said, "Go away." I decided that he did not wish to see us. As I turned back to my car I heard a buzzing sound which was the gate opening. I then assumed that his "go away" meant to stand back so the gate can open. That was the case so we proceeded up his beautiful driveway for about a hundred yards and came into a courtyard where he was standing to greet us. He was a tall distinguished looking gentleman and was well turned out. I then assumed that his "I'm busy" meant that he would be busy preparing to meet us in style.

He was very gracious and was most interested to hear of my part in the liberation of his part of the world. He showed us through the castle/chateau and posed with Muriel for photos. I asked him how he dealt with the German Army while they controlled that part of his country. He told me that as he was the leading citizen of the area they needed him in order to help administer some semblance of local government while they were there. They occupied his chateau until our Force drove them out of his village. Like many patriotic Frenchmen he chose to wait it out as best he could knowing that eventually the conquerors would be gone.

After our unit passed though that area we did not meet any resistance on our way to Nice, the major city on the Riviera. We soon found ourselves faced with crossing the Var River. It was more or less the west border of the city of Nice. Cannes, Juan-les-Pins and Cap d'Antibes were then towards our rear, having been cleared by forces working on our right flank. On approaching the Var River our headquarters group joined up with Colonel Jack Akehurst, our regimental commander. He asked our reconnaissance sergeant, Luther Tilley, and myself to accompany him for the entry into Nice. Through radio contact he had learned that Nice was then pretty well in the hands of the FFI, (French Forces of the Interior) mostly volunteer civilians who were able to show their stuff when the Allies were at the gates of their towns and cities.

The Var flows down from the Alps and into the sea just west of the Nice Airport. As we approached the river we saw that the main bridge leading into the city had been partially destroyed by the retreating enemy. One span of it was sagging into the water. We picked our way across on the roadway which was still hanging together by the steel reinforcements in it but about ten yards of it was under a foot or two of water. We were met on the east side by a delegation of city officials who had brought a very official looking black open car in which they proposed to drive us into their city.

Colonel Akehurst sat in the front seat beside the driver and Tilley and I perched on the front fenders with our sub machine guns. There didn't seem to be any danger of enemy action at the time but it was prudent to keep our eyes on roof tops as we did going into Rome. The French certainly had everything under control. The streets were lined with crowds of flag waving people, some of them offering flowers and others wine. We were treated to accolades which were more deserved by our many friends who had been killed or wounded on their journey of liberation. It was a humbling yet fantastic experience I shall never forget.

Our first duty was to our host of several days past, Monsieur Poteau, for whom we had promised to deliver a message to the staff of his hotel in Nice. He owned l'Hotel Britanique, which was located right on the avenue on which we were entering the city. Our present hosts obligingly stopped their car in front of the hotel while we delivered the message that all was well with the folks at Roquefort-les-Pins. We proceeded from there to city hall where we met his worship the mayor and several others who made us feel like real heroes. It was pandemonium as champagne was offered and much handshaking and kisses on both cheeks as only the French can manage.

Tilley and I were dispatched to seek out battalion headquarters. They had followed us on foot. We soon located Major McFadden and our people and we all made our way to our allotted sector which was the north flank of the city up in the high priced real estate area. We pulled into an imposing looking villa which perched on a hill overlooking a well-treed orchard. We parked our jeep in the courtyard and were welcomed into the house by a middle aged lady who spoke perfect English. It turned out that she was a widow who had lived in California until she and her late husband moved to Nice just prior to the war. She was most hospitable and welcomed us to use her beds and bathrooms as we saw fit. We enjoyed an evening meal with our rations and her wine, while sitting at her dining room table.

The next morning I went out to get my shaving gear from the jeep and was met in the courtyard by an unkempt looking bunch of "freedom fighters." I would classify them as a bunch of bandit opportunists after listening to a tirade from their leader. He stepped up to me and pounding his chest he demanded that we hand over the woman who owned the villa to him and his band. He stated that she had collaborated with the officers of the German occupation by entertaining them in her home. I knew by now that what they had in mind was the treatment given many of the women who had fraternized with the Germans. They would strip her naked and shave her head and lead her down the streets with a rope around her neck to show everyone what a poor Frenchwoman she was.

I looked around and noted that there were about ten or twelve men in his group. A couple of them had a machine gun set up and aimed at her back door from down in the orchard. Summoning most of the French I had learned in high school I suggested that they were indeed a brave bunch of Frenchmen. I asked if it took so many armed men to subdue one little old lady. I also suggested that there were "Beaucoup des Allemands dans les montagnes." They looked around at each other and had a pow-wow and decided to take off for greener pastures. I had really sweated that one out. We never saw those guys again, but I ran across the woman at a later date. I spotted her sitting at a sidewalk cafe in Nice about a month later. She had learned what I had done for her that morning and asked me to join her for a drink. I congratulated her on still having her hair.

It was difficult to believe that anyone had much choice as to who they may or may not entertain given the nature of the German occupation of Europe. Some of the things they inflicted on the populace were next to unspeakable. At one place we had stopped for a break near Cagnes a woman from a nearby home came over and offered us some fresh fruit and vegetables. She related a story about how the Germans had removed her husband's trousers and had run him down the street so that everyone could see that he was circumcised. They thought that he was a Jew, as if Jews were the only people practicing circumcision. He was subsequently able to prove that he was a good Catholic.

Just prior to moving out of the suburbs of Nice I was witness to a most idiotic tragedy unfolding before my eyes and couldn't act fast enough to prevent it. Across the street from me as we prepared to move out I saw a couple of very young replacements kibitzing about how many enemy soldiers they had shot. It appeared to be just the juvenile banter of kids who had one or two drinks too many. One of the fellows handed his .45 Colt pistol to his buddy and taunted him, daring him to shoot him. The lad who took the proffered pistol pointed it at his buddy's shoulder and squeezed the trigger. The gun went off severing the backbone of his friend. He died immediately.

It was all the more serious as a military problem in our international Force as the lad who shot his friend was an American and the fellow he killed was a Canadian. The American lad was immediately arrested and taken to a detention centre in Nice. I was involved in transporting the body to a location designated as such by a graves registration unit. We had to get a stretcher from our medics and load the body onto the back of our jeep. It was difficult to find the location of the unit in question but we finally arrived there. What a grisly business it was to try to explain what had happened. Fortunately I didn't have to attend the international court martial which was held some month or so later. I thought I had witnessed the ultimate degree of idiocy when the fellow on Kiska tried to detonate the mine he found on the beach with his entrenching tool. I was wrong.

There was no doubt that the enemy had completed his withdrawal from Nice and environs. We had moved out as far as the village of Drap, just a few miles east of Nice. We spent the night there and the next morning Major McFadden organized a patrol to proceed eastwards into the mountains. The patrol consisted of one of our Armored half-tracks with the 75 mm. gun and a section of men to ride in its truck-like back. I and my driver were to follow the half-track in our jeep. I think my driver's name was Hoskins. I called him "Switchback" because of the way he managed the many sharp curves we encountered in crossing the south of France.

After a brief breakfast of hard rations and coffee we mounted up and set off up a gravel road into the mountains, the armored vehicle leading. Little did we know that three of the men we had enjoyed our brief breakfast with would not live to have lunch. They were the enlisted men in Lieut. Gettinger's artillery forward observer group of the 607 Pack Artillery Regiment. We had gone about five or six miles when we rounded a hill and were facing a concrete bunker about a half mile ahead of us to one side of the road where it went through the pass. Sgt. Cain, the commander of the half-track ordered his gunners to zero in on the bunker with one round of high explosive. They fired point blank and hit it right in the gun port. When the dust had settled we proceeded cautiously up the road towards it. As there was no answering fire we assumed it was either empty or that the round we had sent their way had put them out of action.

We rushed up the road and stopped short of the bunker. We were on a gravel road so there was a good chance that it would be mined in a location like the pass. Sgt. Cain had his men dismount and with their bayonets they probed the gravel with great care. They were able to locate and dig out about eight or ten Teller mines. Each of which contained enough explosive to disable a tank. Being satisfied that there were no more mines in the road we proceeded eastwards.

If it is possible to describe a combat patrol as exciting, and extremely interesting from a tourist's point of view, that one certainly qualified. The scenery was enchanting to say the least. Our road took us through a couple of fairly short tunnels, and along some narrow ledges with a great view of valleys many feet below. We eventually rounded a bend which exposed a scene right out of the Fairy Tales. We hadn't yet caught up with any of the fleeing enemy so could enjoy the scenery. There ahead of us in stark relief, against a panorama of morning mists, stood the very picturesque village of Ste. Agnes. It was perched near the top of a small mountain about a half-mile distant. I have since learned that it is the highest village in Southern France.

As we raced towards the village someone spotted a column of German soldiers fleeing down into the valley on the road south of Ste. Agnes which leads to Menton, a city on the coast. Our patrol stopped and we commenced firing our small arms (rifles and submachine guns) at the enemy column. They proved to be a difficult target as they were too far away for our firepower to be effective. The crew on our 75 mm. could not depress the gun sufficiently to zero in on them as they were several hundred feet below us.

After a hasty discussion we decided to press on into the village to see if any of the enemy remained there. We were soon inside the village and surprised a German sergeant who was trying to destroy some papers from his office. We took him prisoner and loaded him into our jeep. With our prisoner, "Switchback" and I sped back down the road we had just come up hoping to find Lt. Gettinger and his party so that we could get some howitzer fire directed at the fleeing column below. Howitzers had the ability to lob shells over a mountain and land on targets that flat trajectory guns couldn't reach.

We received a terrible shock when we reached the place where we had cleared the mines from the road. There was a huge crater in the road near the bunker and the only thing recognizable near the crater was the twisted front bumper of a jeep, bearing the markings of our 607 Pack Artillery. The remains of the jeep and its crew were scattered about among the rocks and bush on both sides of the road. We had begun meeting troops on foot by then and they pointed back down the road to an ambulance which was heading back towards our base at Drap.

They had learned that the only survivor of the explosion was the officer. We were later to learn that he, seeing the mines that were stacked beside the road, had stopped his jeep and told his crew to wait while he double checked the road for mines. It's entirely possible that they may have backed up over a mine we had missed. Their weight added to ours may have been all it took to sever the copper wire in its trigger mechanism. It bothered me for weeks afterwards that on such a fragile thread as the thickness of a copper wire my life may have depended.

We drove through the crater and continued to carry our prisoner back down the road to someone we could hand him over to for interrogation.

After driving a couple of miles we caught up with the ambulance. As we closed on it we could see the bandaged head of Lt. Gettinger staring out the rear windows of the vehicle. He had been wounded by the explosion which killed his three men. As the ambulance pulled in to the base which was established at Drap we drove in right behind it. I realised too late that we should have by-passed the ambulance and taken our prisoner further back than the aid post at Drap. The rear doors of the ambulance flew open and out charged a very distraught man whc had just seen his three best friends blown to bits in front of his eyes.

Before we could react he had our prisoner by the throat and would have killed him with his bare hands except for the intervention of several of us including Major Jerry McFadden. We managed to hustle the prisoner to another venue before anything further happened to him. We never saw Gettinger again. The poor man had a lot of grief to overcome as his group was a closely knit bunch who had been together throughout the war.

As a post script to that episode I must relate the following: My wife Muriel, and I have visited the scene of that mine incident twice since the war ended. I guess there was something about it that has touched me more deeply than most of the close calls that I had during the war. It is almost as if I have been given these added years for a purpose ordained by a power beyond our understanding. The first time I was back there was during a motor coach tour of Europe in 1987. We had a two day stopover in Beaulieu, a town between Nice and Monte Carlo. During our stay there we took a train to Menton and hired a taxi to take us up the mountain to Ste. Agnes.

We then drove west on the road towards Drap, which is now paved, so we were not worried about mines. We found a spot at which the French had built a small shrine constructed of a large calibre rusted artillery shell and other bits of rusted military hardware, which, I assumed, was in honour of the three American lads who were killed there. We took some pictures and had our driver take a picture of us as well.

When we returned to the same spot in a car we had rented in Paris in 1994 we had more time to examine everything in detail. The Col de la Madonne, as it is now known, appears to be a popular picnic area for the locals. I met some of them and explained what really happened there fifty years earlier. The inscription welded on a plate on the cairn indicated that the jeep was destroyed by an artillery shell. Anyone not knowing the details as I had witnessed them could very easily have come to that conclusion. Upon examining the cairn and statuary more closely than on my previous visit it struck me forcefully that the Madonna and Child depicted by the rusty hardware was composed of pieces of a destroyed jeep. I realised with an emotional shock that it may well have been made from the remains of my own jeep had fate so chosen.

Following the handing over of our prisoner to a Prisoner of War Compound near Drap I returned to our battalion H.Q. which was getting ready to move out on foot towards the small city of Menton below us on the coast. We arrived in the seemingly deserted town several hours later and it was almost spooky to wonder where all the people were hiding. I since learned that our second regiment had recently passed through and had taken a few prisoners who remained behind to surrender of their own free will. The second had passed on east to hold the line from the Franco-Italian border at the coast and well up into the mountains on their left. The sector we were eventually to man was from their left flank to several miles northward, in terrain which did not give us the high ground that second regiment enjoyed.

I and several of my squad cautiously made our way into one of the larger hotels on the main street of Menton. The lobby appeared empty until a meek looking clerk came out of the inner office and greeted us with "Guten tag mein herren." We hastily informed him that we were Americans. He appeared skeptical at first and finally relaxed with the knowledge that we were trying to tell him that the Germans had left.

In order to travel from west to east in that part of France it was necessary to use the lower coastal routes from time to time. There were very deep valleys between high mountain ridges which ran down to the coast every two or three miles. Such a coastal road led us through Menton. As our battalion caught up with us we elected to set up our headquarters in the north end of the town to be closer to the sector that our three companies were to occupy. Our three line companies were given the area from Castellar north to Mount Grammondo.

During the several weeks that our Battalion Headquarters was in Menton we were constantly targetted for either mortar or Howitzer fire by the observers on the mountains above us. On one occasion I was driving on some errand to Castellar and had to go through the centre of Menton to connect with the road which ran up the steep slope to that village. As we proceeded into the centre of town a heavy barrage fell upon the district we were passing through. Someone came out of a building on our right screaming for medical assistance. A civilian in the building had been severely wounded in the back by shell fragments. We had a stretcher on the back of our jeep and were able to load the man into it. We had to lay him face down as his back was so badly lacerated. By the time we arrived at our regimental aid post we found that he had died. His face had been depressed in the canvas of the stretcher and his blood had filled the depression. He may have drowned in his own blood. It was also possible that the wound was serious enough to end his life.

On another occasion I again had a miraculous escape that I found hard to understand. My jeep driver and I were taking a couple of replacements (newly arrivals) from Menton up to Castellar and as we traversed the lower coastal road a heavy barrage of shells landed all around us, one of them hitting the limb of a tree which overhung the road just as we were passing beneath it. As it exploded we seemed to be at the very centre of the blast. I directed the driver to pull over and we all scrambled out of the jeep and into the doorway of a nearby building.

When the shelling stopped we took stock of our situation. Of the four of us who were in the jeep only one man had received a wound. It was a very minor wound as a small piece of shell fragment had lodged in his lower jaw and was easily extracted later by our medical personnel. We attempted to start the jeep and found it to be fairly well riddled with shrapnel holes, including the engine compartment. One piece of shrapnel had severed the distributor from the engine block. On examining the road under the tree which had been the source of detonation we could make out the outline of our jeep in the blacktop of the street. The shrapnel had left an almost photographic impression surrounding where the jeep had absorbed most of the shrapnel. A miracle?

While our headquarters was located in the bottom of the valley north of Menton we took turns mounting guard during the night in case an enemy patrol might stumble on our location. Their observers on the mountain top probably had our location figured as a location of some note as there was plenty of traffic coming and going from our building. Whoever it was who had the guard duty at any given time was to use my Thompson sub-machine gun as weapon of choice.

One night that Tommy Cole was on guard and the rest of us were playing cards or listening to the radio we heard a staccato burst of fire outside our front door. We assumed that Tom had seen at least an enemy patrol until I noticed that my "Tommy Gun" was still leaning against the wall near the front entrance. I grabbed my gun and was heading for the door when Tom came in holding his very bloody left hand in his right.

He quickly explained that he was cocking the action on his .45 Colt pistol and as the first round entered the firing chamber the pistol fired the complete magazine of seven slugs at what appeared to be full automatic. He had dropped the now empty pistol on the ground. When it began to fire he tried to hold it down with his left hand but the recoil made it buck right through his grip causing two or three of the shots to penetrate his hand. It all happened so fast. It was a classic case of misfire as something in its mechanism stuck allowing it to empty the magazine. It was only a semi-automatic but fired like a machine gun.

We bandaged his hand and loaded him into our jeep and sped him down through town to our regimental aid post. He recovered from those wounds about a month later and was able to use his hand again. A week or two after that episode we moved our headquarters up to the village of Castellar where we occupied the second floor of an empty building. During our time in Castellar we more or less acted as a supply depot and communications centre for our battalion. Our companies were holding a line about half way up the mountain to our east. They and we continued to be targets for the artillery and mortars on the other side of the border. It was at Castellar that I became familiar with the mule skinners of the American Army. A detachment of them and their mules were stationed in a large stable at the north end of our village. They earned their keep in the dangerous job of ferrying food, water and ammunition up to our companies.

From that day on we had only sporadic contact with the enemy. As our mission was to help drive them out of France in our sector it appeared that our task was almost accomplished. However, our third regiment, which was to our north, still had some very tough obstacles to overcome. The enemy had holed up in the well fortified village of Castillon a few miles up the valley from our position in Menton. It was to take them several weeks to finally secure that part of the territory. The worst we had to contend with was being under the observation of their artillery spotters. They occupied the top of the mountains to our east which were the Franco-Italian border. They harassed us from time to time with barrages from their howitzers which could lob shells over the mountains with impunity. We had no means of counter battery fire without observers up there to spot their guns.

We had begun a series of patrols from our forward positions to discourage the enemy from occupying his artillery spotting places on the ridge. Those were accomplished under cover of darkness and were sometimes costly in terms of casualties as the enemy had laid many mines in the obvious approaches.

We were getting tired of being the target every time we moved; besides, they were trying to drive us out of Castellar and it would probably just be a matter of time until they landed a shell right on top of our command post. I guess to add to our jitters we knew that our days of combat in the south were nearing an end. No one wanted to be the last soldier killed in the war. Reaching the Italian border, which was our main objective in the South France Campaign seemed to be a signal to let our psychological guards down. That's always a big mistake in a war zone.

Towards the final days of our South of France campaign I was detailed by Major McFadden to accompany a combat patrol composed of a platoon of our fifth company. We were to climb the mountain under cover of darkness and attempt to shut down the artillery observation post which the enemy had established there. I arrived at number six platoon's bunker just before darkness set in. They were occupying one of the concrete emplacements that the French had built as part of the Maginot Line South.

In order to limit the chance of stepping on any mines we chose a tortuous route through a very rocky approach to the high ridge above us. The going was slow as we didn't wish to make any undue noise or dislodge too many rocks. Shortly before the first glimmer of dawn we were in a location that could be called a small saddle. We had a vantage point where we could see a trail which appeared to lead up to where we thought the enemy had his forward observer post. We were able to lay in wait pretty well surrounded by some very large boulders reminiscent of so many ambushes we have seen in Western movies.

Before too long we spotted seven or eight of the enemy making their way up the trail to their outpost. They appeared to be a supply detail and one of them, likely their medic, carried a folded stretcher. We held our fire until they were well within range and then we opened up on them. One of them was wounded and fell to the ground. The rest threw down their weapons and dived for the ground. The bravest of them cautiously stood up with his hands raised high and was soon followed by the rest. Their medic administered first aid to his wounded companion and had him loaded on the stretcher. We felt like we had done a fair night's work as we made our way back down our side of the mountain with our prisoners.

We weren't home free yet. When we had almost reached the relative safety of our lines we began to be shelled with either howitzer or mortar rounds. The guy who was denied his supplies as we hijacked his party must have been a real mean dude as his directed fire could very easily kill or wound some of his former buddies. As it happened no one in our whole party was injured as the rounds were all off target.

Our patrol and prisoners managed to reach one of the concrete bunkers from which we began our foray. We got on the phone and called for intensive counter battery fire to neutralize the enemy guns while we made our way down to battalion headquarters. It was shortly after our patrol that the enemy appeared to have abandoned all thoughts of manning his outpost on top of the ridge. We probably had taken the only personnel they were able to spare for supply detail.

One of the few times I had any dealings with Colonel Edwin A. Walker (who had taken over command of the Force from General Frederick) was when we arrived at the road which ran to our headquarters in the bottom of the valley. He seemed anxious to have our prisoners interrogated to find out what plans they may have for remaining in their positions in Italy. (As a matter of interest, Walker, later a major general and retired, was living in Dallas, Texas when J.F.Kennedy was shot. I recalled reading a news item in *TIME* magazine in April of 1963 that someone had taken a shot at General Walker as he sat in his living room. The bullet was reported to have lodged in the wall only inches from his head. During the many enquiries of the Warren Commission which examined the Kennedy assassination in detail it was stated by Marina Oswald, Lee Harvey's widow, that it was Oswald who had taken a shot at Walker in April of 1963. As the Kennedys were barely on speaking terms with Walker, Bobby Kennedy, the Attorney General, refused the request of the Dallas police at the time to have the F.B.I. investigate who was trying to kill Walker.)

On the 24th of November, 1944 our whole unit was replaced on the front by the famed Japanese-American 100th Battalion. We moved back to the Loup River valley west of Nice near the village of Villeneuve-Loubet. Our final days as an international special strike force were at hand.

According to figures released by Colonel Burhans, who wrote the history of our Force, we had suffered over 2300 casualties, including over 400 killed and missing. By then a lot of the people who made up our ranks were replacements from both our Armies. They had neither the benefit of the training in Montana, Virginia, nor Vermont, nor the experiences of the Aleutian nor most of the Italian campaigns. It was a bitter-sweet day for us on December the 5th when the Force held its last parade. We all lined up by company and regiment and with ceremony marched past as Colonel Walker took the salute. Our Force Colours were lowered as our Adjutant read the deactivation orders and were sheathed in their casing.

The Canadians among us were ordered to fall out and form up as one unit. That was the first time since joining the Force that we had ever done so. It soon became apparent to many of us that people we thought to be Canadians were in fact Americans and vice versa. It was a memorable occasion, not without some moments of regret.

CHAPTER 21

Return to the Canadian Army

The next evening our Canadian contingent boarded trucks for the long ride to Marseille where we boarded a French liner by the name of Ville D'Oran. After the usual waiting we slid out of the harbour under the frowning edifice made famous in the classic tale, *The Count of Monte Cristo*. It was the menacing Chateau D'If.

The voyage to Naples was an idyllic cruise until our second night out when we ran afoul of the worst storm I have ever encountered at sea. We were sleeping in hammocks two decks down from the promenade deck when the ship rolled so far to starboard that all of our hammocks swung up and touched the ceiling. We seemed to hang there for several seconds as if the ship was trying to make up its mind whether to turn completely over or to right itself. During those very tense moments the mess gear (tin buckets and plates) which were stored in shelving along the side of our compartment, came shooting across the area with a great clatter. A very scary moment indeed.

When we docked in Naples while we were waiting to disembark I managed to speak to one of the crew of the ship about the storm we had encountered. He said that the instruments on the bridge showed the ship would have turned turtle if it listed one more degree towards starboard. The funnels had actually dipped in the sea. He didn't mind admitting that everyone in the wheel-house was scared witless. Although I have never been very superstitious I may have been even more frightened than I was if I had stopped to realize that the Ville D'Oran was the thirteenth "ship" which I had sailed on during the war.

After going ashore we were loaded into trucks again for a reasonably short trip through the night to billets in the town of Avelino, about ten miles north of Mount Vesuvius. At Avelino we were divested of our American uniforms, being allowed to keep only our treasured and distinctive parachute boots. We spent a few hours every day being reintroduced to Canadian Army commands and drill. We also needed to have our new Canadian uniforms adjusted and decked out with our various insignia and chevrons of rank. It was quite a transition. One small compensation was that we were issued the cherry berets of the Airborne regiments.

We were in Avelino for Christmas of 1944. We spent a very unusual Christmas morning as we were all called out of our billets to participate in what the army referred to as an "Identification Parade." Apparently one of the local senoras complained to the authorities that she had been sexually assaulted on Christmas Eve. As we stood at attention in three ranks, she and the inspecting officer made their way past, pausing in front of each of us for the lady in question to have a good look into our stoney faces. The thought must have been common among us, "What if we all look the same to her—are we playing a game of Italian (Russian) Roulette?" It was difficult to consider her in the role of a sex object. Poor woman. In all fairness to her she did not put the finger on any of us. Whew!

During the week that followed we were trucked back to Naples where we boarded a well built ocean liner, the Arundel Castle. We soon learned that our destination was to be the British Isles. That turned out to be one of my more interesting voyages, probably second only to the trip to New York on the Queen Mary. I recall the the accommodations were more than adequate, the food was good, and the ship was indeed a thoroughbred in every respect. She behaved well in all conditions of wind and storm.

We put in to harbour at that most famous of British outposts, Gibraltar. Our timing could not have been better as it was New Year's Eve. We were anchored in the vast harbour amidst an amazing flotilla of ships of war and commerce. We had the better part of a day to admire the famous logo of the Prudential Life Assurance Company, the "Rock" itself. As we were in relatively spartan quarters on board a troop ship there did not at first appear to be any great way to celebrate the advent of a new year.

However, at about five minutes to midnight several explosions got our attention and we hurried out on to the decks. For the next half hour or so we were privileged to witness and hear what had to be the world's finest New Year's Eve celebration. The crews of all the shore installations and the ships anchored in the harbour tried to outdo one another as searchlights and anti-aircraft guns began to sweep the skies above the "Rock." Sirens and fog horns joined the chorus of gun fire to make the sound and light show a never-to-be-forgotten event. The tracer bullets and shells resembled strings of red hot beads being pulled up into the sky. The anti-aircraft shells provided a special effect as they exploded when they reached the desired altitude. From time to time we could hear shell fragments dropping onto our deck. (And I had left my steel helmet back by my bunk.) It made one wonder who was paying for all the fun and how much—but not for long.

The next day we sailed out of "Gib" in a convoy. We were going to be in the North Atlantic for several days and it was still the territory of the "U" Boat packs. There was still a war going on. As we passed through the Straits of Gibraltar the sea was alive with porpoises. They were so thick "you could almost get out and walk on them" as they frolicked in our bow waves to lead our ship through to the Atlantic.

We had fairly smooth sailing until we entered the Bay of Biscay about a day after leaving Gibraltar. We witnessed some of the hugest waves I have ever encountered as our stout ship headed into them. Fortunately the wave action was at right angles to our forward direction so the ship could plow into them without any noticeable sideway rocking. As it was, each oncoming wave presented a mountain of green translucent water which the ship nosed square-ly into, taking tons of it over the foredeck.

We had several Corvettes as escorts during the run from Gibraltar to Scotland and during the mountainous seas we encountered in the Bay of Biscay about the only parts of them that were visible were their masts and occasionally a funnel. A day or two later we came alongside one of them as we sailed in the very calm waters of the Irish Sea and were able to converse with them by shouting. They told us that during the heavy going they hadn't a hot meal for several days as the cooks couldn't control the equipment in their galley. They lived on sandwiches and tea only.

For the second time I sailed into the mouth of the Clyde which is the harbour nearest Glasgow. The first time was in 1941 aboard the Empress of Russia. It was also the same harbour in which I boarded the Queen Mary for the voyage to New York in 1942. It was good to be landing in a friendly country again where some form of English was spoken. After disembarking in Gourock we boarded a train which, with several changes, took us to that small city hated by most soldiers, Aldershot. It was while at Aldershot that I was recommended for officer training and subsequently posted to a pre-OCTU school at Wrotham, in Kent. Those of us who were not sent to officers training were absorbed into the First Canadian Parachute Battalion and, following a brief course in Canadian weaponry and parachute drill, were dispatched to join the regiment already in contact with the enemy near the Rhine River.

At the completion of the pre-OCTU course we were dispatched to a university of our choice for several weeks of general theory. I can't help but think that the Army's rationale for sending us thus was a token attempt to try to give us a final bit of polish which may help us to feel more comfortable in an officer's mess. I chose to go to Oxford and my college of choice was Baliol. It was while I was in Oxford that the war against Germany ended with the complete collapse of their criminal government and war machine.

As we were still at war with Japan our celebrations were tempered by the knowledge that those of us still in uniform would someday soon be sent to fight in the jungles of Southeast Asia. On our return to the next phase of officer school at a branch of Sandhurst known as 161 OCTU our training was intensified in an attempt to prepare us for whatever we would likely encounter in the Far East.

By the first of August, 1945 we had almost completed our qualifications for becoming officers. On the 6th we received news of the bombing of Hiroshima. There was little doubt that the war with Japan had only days to wind down. I can still recall the intense relief we felt in knowing that we now had a very good chance of living through a war which had claimed so many of our friends and relations. The men in my class at OCTU were given several choices. We could be commissioned and spend some time in the army of occupation in Germany; we could sign up for a period of duty in the permanent peacetime army, or we could be discharged and become what most of us dreamed of becoming—civilians. I chose the latter. I figured that a civilian was one rank higher than a five star general.

Berths on homeward bound ships were allotted on the basis of points earned. I had acquired a lot of points because of my time in the service, number of months overseas and weeks at various fronts. I was among the earlier ones to be awarded a spot on a Canada bound ship. Before long I found myself aboard the third largest ship afloat, the Ile de France. After departing from Southampton we were just short of the western tip of Britain when all motion of the ship ceased. A faulty bearing had to be replaced before our voyage could continue. Luckily the U-Boats were no longer a problem.

Our crossing was very smooth with no storms and no worries about being torpedoed. I was fortunate to be given VIP treatment by a fellow who was in charge of the ship's hospital. He spotted my shoulder flash (FSSF) as I boarded the ship in Southampton. He asked me if I knew his son who served in the Force. As luck would have it I did know his son quite well. He then directed me to what turned out to be a private stateroom in the hospital area. As we progressed on the voyage it became plain that I was indeed fortunate as there appeared to be "standing room only" in most areas of the very crowded ship.

No hammock below decks for this voyage. I didn't even have to go down and line up for meals as he had arranged for same to be delivered to our quarters as if I was a star patient in his all but empty sick bay. He and his staff of nurses and orderlies were most congenial hosts as he portrayed me as some kind of hero who had looked after his son during our battles, which, of course was a lot of bunk. It was more than likely the other way round. His son was a medic.

After about six days of smooth sailing we entered Halifax harbour. It was a very emotional moment for a lot of us who may have given up hope of ever seeing Canada again. Upon siding up to the pier in Halifax those of us who had experienced the faces of war-torn Britain and Europe could only stare in wonder at the worry-free faces looking up from crowd below us on the dock. I never realised that there could be such a difference in the faces of people who had not experienced the fear and privations nor the horrors of war. My first impression was that the crowd who looked up from the pier was newly minted from fresh material. It struck me that what we were looking at was really what the previous five years or so had been all about. It somehow made it all seem worth it.

Epilogue

When I finally arrived at my home in Swan River, Manitoba, the same impression was reinforced as I looked into the faces of the young and old alike who were untouched by the madness we had endured. The second night I was home my dear Mother had arranged for a party of sorts to celebrate my homecoming. In one corner of our living room, scarcely noted by me during the excitement of seeing old friends again, sat a stranger I had yet to be introduced to.

She had the freshest and most interesting of all the new faces I was encountering. But that evening I barely had time to say hello to her. She had apparently sat beside my mother in church a week or so prior to my arrival. My mother was always one to make newcomers feel at home whenever she met them, especially if she met them in church. Mother had the foresight to invite her to our party. She was a new primary grade school teacher from the small village of Arden in Central Manitoba. Mother introduced her and another teacher she had also invited as Muriel Gill and Muriel Lintz.

I must admit to being a little slow in the uptake. It must have been a week or two before I really got the names of the two Muriels sorted out enough to decide that it was Muriel Gill that I wished to invite to go to a movie with me. I was more than happy when, after having summoned enough nerve to phone her, she agreed to go to the movies with me. I really didn't get to know very much about her until a week later when we attended a dance together. I found

it hard to believe that anyone as light on her feet and as delicious-
ly soft in my arms and so unspoiled by this world could have survived to be available to a guy like me.

From that day on, the life I had almost thrown away so many
times, took on a whole new meaning. The world became a much
better place than I thought possible. One thing led to another and
by the end of the following March I had managed to scrape together the price of a modest diamond ring. I was able to present it after
convincing that beautiful woman that she should spend the rest of
her life with me. We were married on the 14th of August, 1946.

Our life together was to last for forty-eight years during which
I was privileged to share so very much of this world's joys, and yes,
a few of its sorrows with her. We managed to raise five children—
four daughters and one son. As the years sped by too quickly the
very best memories are the ones I find the hardest to recall. The
urgency of making a living seemed to blot out a lot of the really
important things that one should remember such as the first steps
of a child, the family picnics, days at the beach and Christmas din-
ners. It is difficult to find the mental pictures without the aid of
some great photos. Thank heaven for those.

For the greater part of our first forty years together I worked as
a retail car and truck salesman at a General Motors Dealership in
Neepawa, Manitoba. I must have done something right as towards
the end of my career I found myself selling vehicles to the grandchildren of my earlier customers. I consider myself fortunate to
have worked for three generations of the Murray family and in the
countless friends and good customers it was my privilege to meet
through the car business.

Although my military experience had all been with the army
I was asked, in 1952, to take command of our local Air Cadet
Squadron. I was happy to serve in that capacity for ten years and
enjoyed my work with the boys who came through our ranks year
after year. I also enjoyed my contacts with the various R.C.A.F.

The author as C.O. of Number 9 Neepawa Squadron, Royal Canadian Air Cadets, 1952 to 1962.

Photo by Eric F. Holland.

stations nearby which acted as our parent units. While they were still operative in the fifties and early sixties they were R.C.A.F. Station MacDonald, R.C.A.F. Station Rivers and R.C.A.F. Station Southport of Portage la Prairie. Many of the lads who had their first training in our squadron went on to become airline captains and one chap in particular made the army his career and at the time of writing (1996) is now Major General Raymond Crabbe.

During the decade of the sixties I managed to qualify as a private pilot, (single engine, land.) That, with the expertise of the fine instructors of the Brandon Flying Club and their very forgiving Cessna aircraft. During my flight training in the winter of 1960-61 I flew over the east side of the Riding Mountain National Park and first viewed the ski runs which were being prepared for what was to become the Mt. Agassiz Ski Area. Coinciding with that experience I read a call for tender in the *Winnipeg Free Press* asking for bids to construct and operate a chalet and ski lifts in that area.

Thus began another exciting period of my life. Without leaving my job as a car salesman, I managed, with the help of Jack Taylor and R.T. (Bill) Robinson, to cobble together a small company

The author at
Mt. Agassiz Ski Area.

Photo by Eric F. Holland.

known as Agassiz Enterprises Limited for the purpose of bidding on the ski area construction and operation. Jack Taylor was the president of the Winnipeg Ski Club and Bill Robinson was a local Life Insurance salesman and a syndicated columnist of some note in game and fish circles. I was to serve as the first president of the small company and as such assumed many of the organizational duties. After a rather hectic period of dealing with architects, lawyers, surveyors, engineers, bankers (always the bankers) and National Parks Officials we managed to be awarded the tender to go ahead with construction as planned.

That venture was enhanced by the personal enjoyment that my family and I got out of being involved in the ski business. It was always a thrill to ride up on the T-bar and survey the slopes and the crowds of people who were enjoying themselves. Agassiz boasted the longest and highest ski runs between the Lakehead and the Rockies and a lot of time and effort went into promoting it in its early years. I really enjoyed being an integral part of it all even though most of the headaches it provided were considered to be mine alone.

In the early days there were seasons when it hadn't snowed until almost the first of December. One year, I think it was 1968, it didn't snow until Christmas day and then only enough to make one wonder if the lifts should be operated with so little snow on the slopes. It was during the snow droughts that I became most involved with bankers in general. I know that at one point my home was in jeopardy of being used as collateral for a large loan. We managed to squeeze by that one safely.

After 1968 the board of directors changed enough that I decided to drop out of the picture as far as management was concerned. I felt that the new board was capable of making any of the major decisions necessary to the life of the company. My wife and I remained shareholders for another ten years or so at which time we sold out our interests but still enjoyed the skiing. In retrospect I am sure that the ski training I enjoyed in the Rockies west of Helena, Montana, had something to do with my becoming deeply involved in an adventure such as the Mt. Agassiz project.

Since retiring from Murray's of Neepawa and the car business in general the lives of my dear wife Muriel and I have been mostly in keeping up with the doings of our children and grandchildren. In August of 1994 Muriel achieved a goal which many of us have vainly sought over the years. She scored a Hole in One at our local golf course. In early October of 1994 Muriel was diagnosed as having cancer in its late stages. After a radical operation and two sessions of chemotherapy she died in her home surrounded by her loving family on the 6th of December of that year.

Muriel's life has had a lasting impact on the lives of many people here in Manitoba. She was the catalyst in the founding of the

Touchwood Park Association here in Neepawa. Touchwood has served the mentally challenged adults in Central Manitoba for over thirty years.

As mentioned on a previous page, we have five children: Marilyn Shinyei lives in Edmonton with her husband Frank and their daughter Marlo. Their older children Julie and Tak are in Vancouver. Son David and his wife Rebecca live in Manchester, Massachusetts. They have twin girls Lisa and Mia and a new son Peter Layton Cottingham. Daughter Karen Cottingham lives in Calgary with her partner, Michael Stephensen. Her daughters, Lia and Megan live with them. Daughter Diane lives in Neepawa, Manitoba, just around the corner from her father. Daughter Joy lives in Winnipeg with her husband, Campbell MacLean, their son Campbell and daughter Joanna.

Muriel and I enjoyed a wonderful bus tour of Britain and Europe in 1987. During a two-day stopover in Rome I hired a taxi and took Muriel down to the old tower of Anzio Beachhead fame where the Mussolini Canal flows into the Tyrrhenian Sea. After a visit with the present owner, who has spent a fortune making it into a very habitable villa, we returned to Rome by way of Castel Gondolfo, on the hill mass surrounding beautiful Lago Albano where we had bivouacked following the liberation of Rome in 1944.

For the past fifty years it has been my good fortune to be able to meet from time to time with many of the men who shared many of my adventures during those hectic times. In 1947 we held the first of many reunions in our favourite frontier town, Helena, capital of Montana. It was agreed at that reunion that our organization would be known as The First Special Service Force Association and would hold annual reunions alternating between a Canadian and an American city each year.

In the intervening years Muriel and I became acquainted with some of the finest people it has been our privilege to know. Aside from the men I actually knew personally during the war we found many new friends among those who were not that close in our widely spread ranks. They and their wives and children became life-long friends.

In 1980 I was honoured by being made president of our international Association. It was the sixth time we held a reunion in Helena. That year Lord Louis Mountbatten had agreed to attend the reunion as our guest speaker. Unfortunately he was killed by an explosive device which was hidden aboard his yacht. He was living in Ireland at the time and became a victim of the ongoing war against British authority. He was asked to be our guest speaker as he had been commander of Combined Operations at one time which included parachute/commando units such as ours.

One of our own officers, Stan Waters, was asked to fill in for the unfortunate Briton and did a most commendable job. His message was most apropos as he was well-acquainted with his audience. Stan Waters went on to become the Commanding General of the Canadian Army. After his retirement he became the first Canadian to ever be elected to the Senate. Sadly, he died of a brain tumour shortly after his election was belatedly ratified by Brian Mulroney.

In the years since the obscenity, the heroism, the sacrifice, the grief, the horrible cost and even the cowardice of the war, I have heard many veterans describe their summation of what it was all about. One of my acquaintances was fond of saying, "It was a hell of a war, but it was better than no war at all." Depending on where and how you were involved that could possibly ring true to some. I always cringed when I heard him utter that silly quip and wondered just how close he got to the actual fighting. And strangely, we have otherwise sane people who would like to rewrite history and deny that a very horrendous series of events really happened.

I have discussed the war with a good friend of mine, Leonard Seaborn of Neepawa. He was taken prisoner by the Japanese during the fall of Hong Kong and was not released for over three and a half very miserable years. He is a very gutsy guy and has less reason than anyone I know to say one good word about the war. His comment the last time I talked to him was, "I wouldn't have missed it for anything, but I sure wouldn't want to do it again." He had discovered something about himself which very few men are able to ascertain. He found that he was able to take the worst that his exceedingly nasty captors were able to dish out. His is a marvelous example of courage under the harshest of conditions.

Leonard's example is one, for which I shall be eternally thankful, that I was not required to follow.

• • •

In April of 1981 while I served as president of our Association I received the following transcript of an interesting excerpt from an address which was delivered in Canada's House of Commons by President Reagan during his visit to Ottawa:

When President Eisenhower spoke from this spot in 1953 he noted his gratitude as Allied Commander in World War II for the Canadian contribution to the liberation of the Mediterranean. This touched my curiosity so I did some research.

I learned that in that war there was something called the 1st Special Service Force—a unique international undertaking at the time. This Force was composed of Canadians and Americans distributed equally throughout its ranks, carrying the flags of both nations. They served under joint command, were taught a hybrid close order drill, and trained together as paratroops, demolition experts, ski troops, and then as amphibious units as well.

The 1st Special Service Force became famous for its high morale, its rugged abilities and tough fighting in situations where such reputations were hard earned. General Eisenhower requested them for special reconnaissance and raiding operations during the

*winter advance up the Italian Peninsula. They were involved in the
Anzio Beachhead campaign and were at the spearhead of the
forces that captured Rome. Its men had the common cause of freedom at their sides and the common denominator of courage in their
hearts. They were neither Canadian nor American. They were
Liberators.*

One may ask, "What impels men to volunteer for special duty,
especially that which could be *harmful to one's health?*" What
indeed!? Could it be the desire to prove something to oneself? Is it
the inducement to be with a company of men in an elite unit? Men
who will no doubt be capable of great things when the chips are
down? Is it the allure of a special uniform and all it promises to
declare about its wearer?

The possibility of wearing a chest full of medals and wings and
other signs attesting to valour were furthest from my thoughts
when I volunteered for parachute training. In examining my own
motives for such a course of action I must admit that, along with
the rest of the two hundred or so from my regiment who volunteered (but were not chosen), the main incentive was likely the
abject boredom with our lot. As infantrymen in the Canadian Army
in Britain in 1942 our living conditions were such that any move
was certain to be an improvement.

More than likely it may have been my selfish instinct for survival. Given our options at the time, there was little doubt that we
were slated to storm the beaches of France at some date in our
future. From my perspective, having had some ship-to-shore training, the thoughts of flying over the well-defended coastline and
dropping silently behind the enemy lines looked like the lesser of
all evils. Results of the ill-fated Dieppe raid confirmed my earlier
decision to seek a change in my direction. Once again fate intervened in my favour. I felt like a sweepstakes winner when I was
selected to train for the airborne regiment.

In one respect the war was the ultimate game of dice. There were very few people who could honestly say that they were the masters of their own fates. Goodness knows, many of us tried in small ways to be just that. Fate was a respecter of skills up to a point. Consider the fighter pilot, who with greater skills than his mates, was able to survive more aerial battles. The longtime veteran of front line duty was proven in many cases to have a far better life expectancy than a newly arrived replacement. Certain skills gained in staying alive were evident as one grew older in the service. On the other hand, a hidden mine or an unseeing artillery shell has spelled the doom of many a skillful soldier, sailor or airman. As with the roller of dice, skill did help to raise the odds of survival by a significant amount. But the ultimate winner, as in any form of gambling, was always "The House", spelled W-A-R.

It is with the utmost of humility that I have penned this tale of survival. For many of my friends our war never ended. It is they who bear the scars of mind and body and have done so courageously. No amount of kind words or loving handshakes can compensate them for the terrible price they have paid and shall continue to pay as long as they live.

I offer this small publication, such as it is, not to glorify war but to relate, in my own small way, some of the events which have changed the world, and the lives, for better or for worse, of so many of the youths of my generation.

A list of the ships on which the author sailed during World War II

Empress of Russia–in convoy from Halifax, Nova Scotia to Greenock, Scotland, October 1941.

Queen Mary–sailed unescorted from Greenock to New York City, October 1942.

William P. Biddle–from Norfolk, Virginia on ship-to-shore exercises in the Chesapeake Bay for a week in May 1943.

Nathaniel Wyeth–sailed from San Francisco to Amchitka, Alaska, July 1943.

U.S.S. Kane–from Amchitka to Kiska for our first rubber boat invasion in August 1943. I am certain that the Caine of mutiny fame was named after this ship.

J. Franklin Bell–sailed back to the U.S.A. in convoy with the world's largest battleship, the U.S.S. Missouri.

Empress of Scotland–sailed unescorted from Newport News, Virginia to Casablanca, Morocco in November 1943.

Thomas Jefferson–sailed from Oran, Algeria to Naples, Italy, November 1943.

LCI 274–sailed from Puzzuoli, Italy to Anzio Beachhead, Feb. 1944.

U.S.S. Cropper–sailed from Anzio to Naples, June 1944.

U.S.S. Rogers–sailed from Santa Maria Di Castelabate to Island of Ponza. Checked out the German garrison, found it empty and returned to S.M.Di C.

U.S.S. Tattnall–sailed from Santa Maria Di Castelabate to Propraino Bay, Corsica, 12 August, 1944, then sailed to make another rubber boat landing in the South of France on 14th August—exactly a year to the day from our similar operation in the Aleutian Islands.

Ville D'Oran–sailed from Marseilles, France to Naples, Italy in December, 1944.

Arundel Castle–in convoy from Naples to Gibraltar, December 1944. We spent a night anchored at Gibraltar. On New Year's Eve we watched in awe as the greatest sound and light show took place. Anti-aircraft guns and searchlights converged over the famous Rock. We sailed the next day, arriving in Greenock several days later.

Ile de France–The war is over. We sailed unescorted from Southampton to Halifax, Nova Scotia in September 1945.

Author's Decorations

Top Row (left to right): Souvenir medallion celebrating the 40th anniversary of the liberation of the south of France; P.P.C.L.I. hat badge; Regina Rifle Regiment hat badge; Silver miniature of special combat knife we all carried; Hat badge of First Cdn. Para. Battalion; Shoulder flash of First Special Service Force; U.S. Army identification tag (called a Dog Tag); Souvenir medallion commemorating the 40th anniversary of the liberation of Rome.

Centre (left to right): Crossed arrows of collar badges, F.S.S.F.; parachute wings of Britain (blue); parachute wings of Canada (white); parachute wings of U.S.A. (silver).

Bottom Row (left to right): 1939-1945 Star; Italian Star; France-Germany Star; Defense of Britain Medal; Canadian Voluntary Service Medal; Victory Medal; 125th Anniversary of Canada Medal; Canadian Forces Decoration (CD); Liberation of France Medal (awarded by France).

Photo by Brian Bailey.